# Chic & Slim

HOW

THOSE

CHIC

FRENCH WOMEN

EAT ALL THAT

RICH FOOD

AND STILL

STAY

SLIM

## Anne Barone

THE ANNE BARONE COMPANY

Chic & Slim:
How Those Chic French Women Eat All That Rich Food And Still Stay Slim
Anne Barone

Copyright © 1997, 2001, 2004, 2009 & 2011 Anne Barone
All Rights Reserved

A Chic & Slim Book
Published by The Anne Barone Company, Texas 76309 USA

ISBN: 978-1-937066-10-9

Third Edition
Book Cover & Design: Anne Barone
Chic Woman Image Copyright © iStockphoto/ karrapa
Eiffel Tower Design: Joyce Wells *GriggsArt*

This book is intended as philosophy and general reference only. It is not to be used as a substitute for medical advice or treatment. Every individual's problems with excess weight are unique and complex. You should consult your physician for guidance on any medical condition or health issue and to make certain any products or treatments you use are right and safe for you. The author and publisher disclaim any responsibility for any liability, loss or risk incurred directly or indirectly from the use or application of any of the contents of this publication or from any of the materials, services or products mentioned in the contents of this book or in supplemental materials published on the supporting website *annebarone.com*.

# Praise for Chic & Slim

Thank you for what you do. You help women to find reason, sanity, and confidence. You help guide them to listen to their inner-voice's needs. You do so much. — LISA

Your books are like mental chocolate truffles. *Merci beaucoup!*
— JUDY

Your book came at the perfect time in my life, especially the chapter about mothers & daughters. That alone will greatly influence my role as a teacher in my household, so thank you!
— ANNA in PHILADELPHIA

As always, your writing is clear and concise and gives wonderful information. I am married to a wonderful Parisian and had the opportunity to live in Paris for almost 3 years and find so many things that you say to be completely true. Thank you for your tireless effort in helping American women find our "French" selves. You are definitely an inspiration.
— ANGELA

Your new book is just a delight. I downloaded a copy and how nice and easy that was. I did not read it all at one sitting as I am wont to do, but stretched it out over a few days. I sat on my chaise looking out to the winter garden, a good cup of tea in hand and just enjoyed a time alone. *Merci.*
— HELEN in TORONTO

You are simply inspiring. Thank you!
— GAIL in AUSTRALIA

dedicated

*avec mille mercis*

to all those

*Chic French Women*

who taught me so much

# Contents

Staying slim is not about
counting calories or fat grams.

Staying slim is not about
exercise exhaustion

Staying slim is really about
Personal Style

# Bonjour!

I could have called this book *How Those Chic French Women Eat All That Rich Food And Still Stay Slim—And How I Used To Eat Diet Food And Count Calories And Stayed Fat.* But a 28-word title seemed a bit much. *De trop*, the French would say.

What you need to know about how chic French women stay slim—and some of the sneaky little ways life in America is making people fatter—is here on these pages.

Yet I must tell you that I am neither physician, exercise physiologist, nutritionist, nor psychologist. I am merely an American woman who grew up fat and miserable. In my mid-20s, I successfully lost weight using techniques I learned from French women. With my American translation of those techniques, I have kept the weight off more than 40 years. No small accomplishment since I live deep in the heart of barbecue and enchilada territory.

The information on these pages is not only for women who want to lose weight. It is for any woman who wants to be chic and slim and in control of her life. Any woman who wants to avoid weight gain provoked by stress or mid-life.

Forget diets. Diets are no fun and don't work. What I learned from French women is that staying slim is not about counting calories or fat grams. Staying slim is not about exercise exhaustion. Staying slim is really about personal style.

Isn't that *fantastique?*

*Anne Barone*

## SLIMNESS

*Maigreur —*

Slimness,

which is

compatible

with perfect health,

should not be

confused with

emaciation.

— *Larousse Gastronomique*

# The Passport to Slim

Those chic French women.

You see them on smart Parisian avenues and Côte d'Azur beaches. Sophisticated. Feminine. Soignée. Possessed of an ultra self-assurance. Whether in the city or on the Riviera, French women always look as if they just stepped off the cover of the French edition of *Vogue*. They radiate that inimitable *je ne sais quoi* we admire—and envy.

How do they do it? we wonder. Yet what amazes us most is that those chic, slim French women *always* seem to be eating. And I don't mean picking at a little salad. They feast on foie gras. They work their way through five-course dinners from the *Terrine de Veau* to the *Mousse au Chocolat*.

In a *salon de thé* they revive themselves from an exhausting afternoon in the boutiques with an éclair and a nice cup of Darjeeling. They drink wine. They sip champagne. Yet all that fabulous French cuisine never seems to put a bulge in their Chanel suits. They always look marvelous in their bikinis—what little of their bikinis they wear.

What's their secret?

*Les aerobics? Certainement, non!* French women don't attend aerobics classes. You don't find chic French women out jogging. Any woman you see running five miles in the Bois de Boulogne is surely a tourist. To jog you must wear running shoes. *Les running shoes ne sont pas chic.* Not chic, at all. A French woman would prefer to have her legs amputated rather than be seen in clunky exercise shoes.

No aerobics. No jogging. So how do those chic French women eat all that rich food and still stay slim?

I can assure you they do not count fat grams. For the average five-course French dinner you need a supercomputer to tally all the fat grams. Say cholesterol to a French woman, and she says, *"Le cholesterol, qu'est-ce que c'est ça?"*

They don't know what it is. In a country where the most beloved sauces are based on egg yolks, butter, and cream, and where super-fatted goose liver is the bread spread of choice, it is probably just as well that they don't know about cholesterol.

Yet, French women have the lowest death rate from heart disease in the world. Their life expectancy is longer than that of American women.

Actually, at the time I'm writing this, the oldest living human on the planet is...that's right...a French woman. She has probably eaten cheese every day of her life. *Formidable!*

I have always found it astounding that French women can eat all that rich food and look so fabulous. How extraordinary that they can eat all that rich food and be healthy, too.

Some people credit the French ability to eat rich foods and stay slim to genetics. I have few, if any, French genes. Yet using techniques learned from chic French women, I lost excess weight and have kept that weight off for more than three decades.

**ONCE UPON A FAT TIME**

I assure you that I was not just temporarily fat when I deciphered French women's system for eating well and staying slim. A chubby toddler growing up in fried chicken, mashed potato, and chocolate cake country, I became a fat child.

By the time I was in fourth grade I was so fat they had to bring in a desk from high school for me. Despite diets and doctor-prescribed diet pills, by high school, at only five feet, four inches—and a female—I outweighed 75 percent of the starting lineup of the football team.

Yet I continually tried to lose weight. Some people seem to have been born with a silver spoon in their mouth. Perpetual dieting made me feel as if I had been born with a calorie counter in one hand and a package of artificial sweetener in the other.

I came to believe the only way to whittle my hip measurement down to normal range would be giving up all the good food I loved, suffering the constant gnaw of hunger, and exercising myself to exhaustion. Not likely.

Following high school graduation I went away to college toting my suitcase filled with size 18. Among all those cute size 5 coeds, I felt like a whale dumped into a gold fish pond. In college I lost some weight, but as graduation came and everyone except me had marriage plans, I found refuge from my single state in coconut cookies and applesauce doughnuts. I treated my insomnia with middle-of-the-night peanut butter and jelly sandwiches. What fat I had lost steadily returned.

Finally, in the autumn following graduation, I fled America, the land of fast food, colas, Fritos pies, a candy bar in every vending machine, and potato chips in every rack. I went to live among the food-obsessed French.

## BONJOUR, FRANÇAIS

Believe me, when you are depressed about your fat state, it is painful to find yourself in the midst of those ultimately chic and slim French women. You who have visited France or a French Caribbean island know exactly what I'm talking about. One look at those women and I wanted to drown myself in the Seine—or any conveniently deep body of water.

Yet before I took any such drastic steps, I made a startling discovery. Those chic, slim French women were always eating! How could this be?

They ate French bread three times a day! My American weight control diets had severely limited bread. Those chic French women regularly drank wine with dinner. American diets prohibited alcohol. Breakfast for French women wasn't breakfast without a steaming cup of *café*. American diets prohibited or limited caffeine. American diets certainly did not allow you to generously douse whole milk or cream in your coffee.

Best of all, those chic French women weren't slaves to an exercise routine. Actually, I rarely saw any of them doing anything rigorously physical. They were too busy sitting around looking gorgeous and perfect.

Now please let me say that I did not immediately embrace the French system. Change is difficult. Close contact with the French made me doubt that their system for weight control might really work for an American. The two nationalities are so different. After all, the French tolerate lousy plumbing. Don't they? They close down the whole country every August and go on vacation. They spend an enormous amount of time sitting around in cafés sipping aperitifs, those drinks that food writer Calvin Trillin has described as tasting like cough medicine. Some aperitifs do; others taste more like horse liniment.

This was the late 1960s. Americans had bigger houses than the French; we had bigger cars. We had supermarkets with multi-acre parking lots while the French were still riding their mopeds to the *marché* carrying their scroungy little shopping baskets. The French might have Camembert, fois gras, and *crème fraîche*. But Americans had instant pudding in ten flavors, two dozen varieties of canned soup, and 45 kinds of breakfast cereal. Never mind that the cereal had the flavor of cardboard, contained little real nutrition, and most of the purchase price went for advertising that brainwashed us into thinking this pseudo-food was better for us than real food.

Yet I could clearly see that even if the French trailed Americans in plumbing, processed food, and household conveniences, those chic French women did manage to eat all that rich food and still stay wonderfully slim.

So I began to observe how and what and when those slim French women ate. I asked questions. I began eating more the way French women did. Before I knew it, I fit nicely into size 7. Eventually size 5.

How ironic that all those years I had conscientiously followed those traditional American diet programs—counted calories and denied myself breads, desserts, and cheese I loved—I had either lost little weight or quickly regained any pounds I lost. But when I began eating and thinking about life and food more the way those chic French women did, I became the slimmest and trimmest of my entire life. *Fantastique!*

## FAT AMERICAN STYLE

Not all Americans have had as happy an experience with weight loss as I. The latest government report indicates that more than two-thirds the U.S. population is overweight. A large percentage of these people are struggling to shed their excess fat. And most, unfortunately, are having about as much success as trying to stuff a size 18 into size 8 jeans.

Keeping the weight off is more difficult than losing it in the first place—despite the billions spent annually on weight control gadgets and programs.

But losing weight is worth whatever it costs. Isn't it? I certainly know that I was fat for almost 25 years, and I have been slim for more than 40 years. And the latter 40 slim years have been far better than those first 25 fat years.

How tired I am of hearing those pious pronouncements that losing weight won't solve all your problems. Nothing, friends, will solve *all* your problems. But losing weight and keeping the weight off solves one major problem: being fat. And when you no longer have to put your time, energy, and money into losing weight, you can devote those resources to finding solutions to what else is complicating your life.

I readily credit French women with giving me the system by which I lost weight and stay slim. Of course I am not unique in gathering good ideas from the French. I came of age in the early 1960s when the chief role model for American females was First Lady Jacqueline Kennedy. Her personal style and taste had been greatly influenced by her travels in France and by her experiences in Paris the year she studied French art and literature at the Sorbonne.

Jacqueline Kennedy's translation of French chic set new standards of cultured elegance in the United States. Her example inspired me to learn the French language and made me more receptive to the lessons French women were teaching me.

Another American woman who made her own unique translation of things French—in her case cuisine—was Julia Child.

When she accompanied her husband to his work in Paris, Julia Child, as we now well know, developed a passionate love for French cuisine. In those years following the Second World War, French cooking was a mystery to most Americans. Cloaked in misty half-myths, it seemed closer to alchemy than to food preparation. The experts assured Julia Child no American woman could ever learn to cook French cuisine. But she proved them wrong. Very, very wrong.

Julia Child mastered French cuisine. She also worked out a method by which American women shopping for American products in American supermarkets, cooking on American appliances in their own American kitchens could prepare that same French cuisine.

Three decades ago Julia Child's first book *Mastering the Art of French Cooking* introduced Americans to the delights of French cuisine.

If Jacqueline Kennedy did more than anyone to raise the standards of taste and style in the United States, Julia Child did more than anyone to raise our standards for good eating.

Someone said Jacqueline Kennedy "classed up our national act." Julia Child surely expanded America's gastronomic horizons. And I benefited greatly from the efforts of both.

French women taught me the art of eating well and staying slim. Since returning to live in the United States I have created my own translations of their system. Shopping in American supermarkets, cooking in my own kitchen (often in my microwave), I can enjoy American—and French, as well as Chinese, Indian, Italian, Mexican, Greek, and Japanese cuisines—without the weight gain that too often accompanies enjoying good food. This book tells you how I do it. And how you also can use these French techniques.

## LE SYSTÈME FRANÇAIS

So how do they do it? Why can French women eat rich food and stay slim, yet American women eat "diet" food and stay fat?

As you will learn in the following chapters, the difference begins with culture. Too, the way French women see themselves as women exerts a strong influence. Even their devotion to *la mode* and personal style keeps them slim. The way they shop and arrange their households keeps the Fat Monster at bay. Unfortunately, the way most American women shop and arrange their households is designed to add about five pounds a year.

You may find it hard to believe, but French cuisine keeps you slimmer than low-fat and sugarless. Truly.

Finally, more than anything else, relationships between French men and women keep them slim and svelte. (Sounds more interesting than 45 minutes a day in aerobics class, doesn't it?)

These days every weight control guru has a place to unload the blame for America's obesity epidemic. But America's fat problem did not begin with the advent of fast food, soft drinks, or processed food. The medical and diet industries are not in a conspiracy to keep us fat.

America's problem with excess fat began when the first colonists stepped off the boat onto the rocky New England soil. I am talking about our Puritan legacy problem. Read on.

# CHAPTER ONE

# La Culture

## PRAGMATISM & PLEASURE & FREEDOM FROM THE PURITANS MAKE THE DIFFERENCE

Blame it on the Puritans. If you wonder why the French, the most food-obsessed people on the planet, can eat all that cream, butter, and egg yolks and struggle far less with excess weight than Americans who dutifully tote home shopping bags of sugarless and fat-free, the answer is: the Puritans. The French never had any; the Americans did. The French had Joan of Arc, Napoleon Bonaparte, Charles De Gaulle, and Brigitte Bardot.

But no Puritans.

Back in 1620 when the Puritans stepped off the Mayflower, they brought with them the intellectual baggage that if something feels good and makes us happy, it is bad. Discomfort and sacrifice are good. The more uncomfortable and unpleasurable something is, the Puritans thought, the better for you. Of course this Puritan philosophy grew out of strong religious conviction.

The French were also religious—in their own fashion. When they wanted to give thanks to God, they built—by hand no less—huge, architecturally magnificent cathedrals. The construction of Chartres, no doubt, burned more calories than all the workout videos ever sold.

For Thanksgiving, the American Puritans fixed a big dinner and ate it. Our annual reenactment of this feast kicks off that part of the year when the average American gains six pounds.

The Puritan legacy was still strong three centuries later when I was growing up in the 1950s. In that small Bible Belt town, drinking alcohol was a sin, smoking was a sin, playing cards was a sin, dancing was a sin, and going to movies was a sin. Any effort to improve your appearance was viewed with suspicion. Once I arrived at a friend's house to find her straitlaced grandmother in a rage. Pointing a damning finger, she demanded, "What do you think about a girl who would go against the will of God?" My friend, it turned out, had straightened her naturally curly hair.

In that Bible Belt milieu, sex outside marriage put you on the fast track to Hell. As for sex in marriage, you weren't supposed to enjoy it. The only sanctioned pleasurable activity was eating. I have witnessed church family night dinners that were food orgies that would have shocked the un-Puritanical French right out of their socks.

The French seek equal pleasure in a well-prepared meal as in a session of passionate lovemaking. Actually the French favor alternating one with the other. But everything in moderation. The French, after all, coined the phrase *la douceur de vivre*, the sweetness of living. Americans coined the phrase "No pain, no gain." The way this works: you go though the pain of dieting. Then you gain it all back.

## THE *NOUVEAUX* PURITANS

In recent decades American Puritanism has undergone an evolution. Activities no longer prohibited for religious or moral reasons, are now on the no-no list as unhealthy. This has given the Puritan mentality an in-road to spoiling our previously okay pleasure in eating. The rules are simple: Anything that tastes good, like grilled steak, enchiladas, fresh-brewed coffee, or peach pie are poisons guaranteed to kill us. Foods such as tofu, bean sprouts, and plain low-fat yogurt are cure-alls promised to put the medical profession out of business and make us all live to 110.

Most new products the food industry has put on the shelves recently carry some (mostly over hyped) health claim. Whatever the fad health ingredient, they add it to everything. During the oat bran craze about the only products in the supermarket without this gritty little addition were laundry detergent and disposable diapers.

These Nouveaux Puritans have studies to back up their claims. But my faith in "studies" is weak. I remember one study that concluded wearing lipstick caused cancer. However, to ingest as much lipstick as they had pumped into those poor little research mice, a human had to *eat* 90 tubes of lipstick per day!

Across the Atlantic the French hear the results of the American Nouveau Puritan food studies, pause a moment from spreading their *pâté de foie gras*, cut a bite of *bifteck*, sip their Beaujolais, and contemplate the cheese tray as they shrug and say, *"Ils sont fous, ces Américains."* They're crazy, those Americans.

## MORE IS BETTER VS. ENOUGH IS BEST

The French system of eating a sensible diet in moderate portions went directly against the philosophy of life with which I grew up. I believed that more and bigger were always better. Much better. Especially when it came to getting your money's worth from a purchase. Almost before I learned the multiplication tables, I figured out how to check the weight on the candy bar wrappers to see which one gave me the most chocolate and nuts for my money. I went for quantity over quality every time. And as a result I grew fatter and fatter.

## THE IMPATIENCE FACTOR

My American impatience contributed to my excess weight when I was a child and teenager. While it's true that my pioneering forebears might never have survived on the frontier if they hadn't had an aggressive get-things-done-in-a-hurry attitude (especially when it came to diving for the storm cellar during tornadoes), that attitude, which I inherited, worked against me whenever I tried to cut back on the amount of food that I ate.

When you eat rapidly, you are more likely to overeat because your stomach lacks sufficient time to send an "all full" signal. Nutritionists also assure us that eating too quickly and failing to chew food well contributes to less-than-optimum metabolizing of food. More of what we eat becomes fat, not fuel.

Eventually I realized that those chic French women could eat all that rich French food and still stay slim because they took small bites and chewed slowly and carefully. Their habit of eating their meals in courses with sometimes fifteen or twenty minutes between courses also helped. (But at first this almost drove me to distraction.) And when I found out that the French routinely closed down offices and schools for a two-hour lunch break, I was dumbfounded. Two hours for lunch! When I was a fatty, I could pick up a hamburger, fries, and a strawberry shake at the take-out and have them eaten before I turned into my driveway.

## CONTINENTAL ETIQUETTE

Even the way French women hold their knives and forks helps keep them slim, I discovered.

Typically Americans eat by the zigzag method. When cutting food on the plate, they hold the fork in the left hand and the knife in the right. After cutting, they place the knife on the plate and switch the fork back to the right hand.

In France, as generally in Europe, the fork is held in the left hand and the knife in the right while eating. Since for most people the right hand is dominant, the fork conveying food to the mouth is held in the non-dominant hand. Holding the fork in the non-dominant hand means you can't put as large a portion on the fork at any one time. (At least, not without seriously risking it will plop back down on your plate. Or worse, in your lap.)

Peas are tricky—unless you do as the French who sensibly eat their *petits pois* with a spoon. Numerous other foods present equally daunting logistic problems. So when I adopted the Continental manner of holding the knife and fork, I was forced to eat more slowly and carefully. Consequently I ate less food.

### INSTANT GRATIFICATION

Another thing that I realized about myself while I was studying French women was how accustomed I had become to instantly gratifying my every twinge of hunger. Like most Americans I see waiting as waste. And Americans are constantly inventing ingenious ways to avoid waiting. We have been highly successful in eliminating waiting for food.

Vending machines, candy counters, convenience stores, fast food restaurants, delis, supermarkets lurk on every corner and line every city street and highway. They gratify instantly the slightest twinge of hunger—with high-calorie, high-fat, highly-sugared, processed pseudo-foods.

I have lived and traveled on four continents, and I assure you in no other country in the world is it so easy to overeat high-calorie foods as in the good old USA.

Since food is so easily available in the USA, adopting French habits such as no snacking, eating only at meals, eating only when seated can counter the tendency to instant gratification.

## DINING À LA FRANÇAISE

When you have grown up accustomed to all this efficiency and instant gratification of hunger, adjusting to the French system can be difficult. In France, I found restaurants were usually open only in those precisely defined hours during which the French dine. Food stores regularly closed between one and four in the afternoon, and snack foods were much less readily available—though every year more American fast food companies open stores in France. Ten years from now it will be interesting to see if the French maintain their superiority in low levels of obesity and heart disease. Or whether the French will have hamburgered and fried-chickened their way to fat thighs and clogged arteries.

As an impatient American I also had difficulty adjusting to the slow pace and formality of French meals. At first I thought the restaurant service was incredibly bad. Then I realized that leisurely eating is the French preference. Dinner invitations to French homes also posed problems. The French usually eat their evening meal around eight. Even young children eat at this time, which means they go to bed almost immediately after the meal. When guests are invited for eight, they probably won't see the dining table until ten.

The French, I found, were not much into hors d'oeuvres. No bowls of chips and dips with the aperitif. You were lucky if there was a small bowl of nuts to fortify you until it was time to dine.

Finally, the French leisurely progression of courses began. Time between courses stretches longer in a home than in a restaurant if Madame herself is cooking. The French believe in absolutely freshly-prepared food—for taste, nutrition, and best digestion. So Madame will likely wait until one course is eaten and the dishes cleared before cooking the next. When food is served in this more paced manner, you are far less likely to overeat.

## NO MIND-ELSEWHERE EATING

Because the French take food so seriously, they don't consume calories in mind-elsewhere eating. When I was fat, I frequently ate with my mind focused elsewhere—frequently on a book or the television screen. The faster the action of the TV program I was watching, the faster I seemed to feed food into my mouth.

Business lunches also generate a lot of mind-elsewhere eating. The French avoid this distracted feeding. They believe that business and meals don't mix. They don't eat at their office desks. That's what that two-hour lunch hour is for. You must leave the office and dine well and properly.

## DESCARTES & CHIC FRENCH WOMEN

In France one does things properly: *comme il faux.* The way it should be done. A ritual order controls activities of everyday life for the French. You do not snack—not because you never feel hungry between meals. You do not snack because that is the French way. You spend hours at the table in serious concentration on your food for the same reason.

All this goes back to the 17th century French philosopher René Descartes. French thinking is Cartesian. Everything neat, orderly, rational. Separation of mind and body. Personal self-control. Mind over matter. Mind over the matter of the temptation to overeat that rich French food.

When I was fat, my attitude toward overeating was definitely not Cartesian. My attitude toward overeating was: Once I pop the top, I can't stop. I can't eat just one salted peanut.

Cartesian thinking influences the French toward moderation and controls temptations to overeat. What prompted me for so many years to seek out food in response to so many needs and emotions?

## THOSE FATTENING ADVERTISEMENTS

One obvious reason Americans overeat is our advertising. American advertising outpaces that of the French in its sophisticated, state-of-the-art psychological manipulation to create craving for food beyond satisfying hunger. French advertising lacks the sexual sell and glamorous promises of American food advertising. One French television commercial that sticks in my mind was for mineral water. The commercial stressed the water's effectiveness against constipation, a malady understandably a problem for anybody who consumes as much bread and cheese as the French. The musical jingle repeated over and over the French word for eliminate. As I said, no *glamorous* promises.

American advertising, on the other hand, bombards us with messages to EAT! It sets out to convince us that, if we eat the advertised food, we will be happier, sexier, more successful, and better at sports. It further suggests, although subtly, that the more of that particular food we eat, the happier, sexier, more successful, and better at sports we will be.

What we are likely to be if we overeat any food is overweight.

Unless we spend our day locked in a dark closet, we can't escape American food advertising. Think about the times you have been cruising along the expressway without a twinge of hunger; then, your peripheral vision picks up the logo of a fast food chain. Suddenly you are ravenous.

But the most forceful food advertising comes via television. Should we be surprised at reports that people who watch commercial television more than four hours a day are more likely to be overweight?

Even if you aren't watching, if you are in sound range, your subconscious laps up those food commercials even when your conscious attention may be elsewhere.

Blame it on advertising. Blame it on the Puritans. The bottom line is that today American culture encourages us to eat more than we want; then, it makes us feel guilty because we overeat. The fat we gain overeating undermines our health and makes us miserable.

French culture, on the other hand, creates a mindset that allows the French to indulge in wonderful food yet regulate their food consumption. As a result, their gourmandry does not render them gargantuan.

Yet more than culture, the way French women perceive themselves as women keeps them chic and slim.

## Praise for Chic & Slim

*Wow! Your recent photo you posted on your website of yourself is wonderful! You look marvelous! You truly practice what you write in your wonderful books. Speaking of your books.... I am SLOWLY reading your Encore book, a chapter each night, because I want to savor every word and enjoy the pleasant time I spend reading each chapter. Truly positive words/thoughts to live by. You are an inspiration to MANY women who pick up your book and read it. Can't wait for the next book!*

*—VICKI in WASHINGTON*

# Thoughts On French Culture

The very heart of French culture is the wonderful *art de vivre* that has evolved over the centuries, nurtured by other cultures, by nature, by the desire for harmonious relations among human beings and to bring pleasure to one's own life and the life of others.

It is that wonderful *je ne sais quoi* we feel when we are in France. You have a lot to say about it in your Chic & Slim books.

Women have played an essential role in the creation of this *art de vivre* and its evolution. It really has little to do with reading and writing which are adjunct functions—or with a technology recording stories and information. It is very useful to be able to read and write, but these activities should not be confused with the living arts themselves.

At the very heart of the art of living are living breathing flesh-and-blood human beings, their personalities, the way they live their lives, the way they talk, the sounds of their voices and their songs, what they say, the way they dress, the way they move, what they are interested in, their gestures, the way they walk and dance and how they interact with others sharing ideas and great conversations—laughing, or being serious and sensitive, and sometimes being charming and a great pleasure to be in their company.

All this can be called an *art de vivre* or culture.

—JANE RATHER THIÉBAUD *Author*
        **Madame Rambouillet's** *Chambre Bleue* **[Blue Room]:**
        **Birthplace of Salon Culture**

# CHAPTER TWO

# L'Art de Femme

## A UNIQUE PERSONAL STYLE WORKS FOR SLIM

The American writer F. Scott Fitzgerald once said to his friend and fellow novelist Ernest Hemingway, "The rich are different from you and me." To this Hemingway reportedly replied, "Yes, they have more money."

Many people believe that the only difference between slim French women and overweight American women is that American women have more fat. Actually the differences are many and profound. Carolyn White writing in the "Paris Fax" column in *Elle* magazine made the observation that French women seem less confused, less tired, less aggressive, less angry than American women. She sums them up in one word: happier.

Ms. White made those observations in the mid-1990s. My impression was exactly the same in the mid-1960s. At that time, however, the gulf between how American women and French women defined their roles gaped less wide than today. Even so, three decades ago I could see how American women's greater fatigue, confusion, discontent, as well as their greater frustration with men sent them seeking comfort in food. Why?

What makes French women see themselves and their role as women so differently?

## LA SORORITÉ DES FEMMES

French women seem to see themselves as members of an exclusive sorority *La Société des Femmes Françaises*. As members, they encourage (pressure actually) each other to be slim and careful about their appearance. Competitive American women sabotage each other's weight loss efforts. If you don't believe this, lose five pounds and see what happens.

In America, as soon as you lose five pounds, someone comments. A woman you believed was your good friend looks you over from your blow dry cut to your mid-heel black pumps and shakes her head. "I knew it," she says in a Doomsday voice, "you are becoming anorexic. Don't you know that's how that singer died?"

You still can't zip last year's jeans and already she tells you that you are starving yourself to death.

Does she really believe you have a life-threatening eating disorder? Of course not. The point is that she has *not* lost five pounds. In what she hopes to pass off as concern for your welfare, she tells you that you are endangering your health. And since you have exhausted your willpower for your diet, that evening you devour two helpings of fettuccine Alfredo and a huge slice of chocolate cheese cake. In another week you have regained the five pounds.

Anyone who has tried to lose weight in America has been a victim of weight loss competitiveness. Myself, many times. French women, on the other hand, offered me sisterly guidance. This helpful attitude toward my weight loss came as a delightful surprise. This ranked somewhere behind other delightful surprises: croissants, éclairs, creamy Gruyère, Beaujolais, the two-hour lunch hour, and the five-course dinner.

I am always surprised when I hear someone refer to French women as snobby. What Americans interpret as snobbishness,

I believe, is French women's extraordinary self-possession combined with the French tendency for civility and formality. (Civility and formality, unfortunately, went out of style in America about the same year as tail fins on cars.) I have been the target of far fewer demonstrations of snobbishness from self-confident French women than from insecurity-ridden, competition-obsessed American women.

Yet I admit French women have a no-nonsense attitude about them. They don't tolerate people who are obsessed with their physical defects and psychological shortcomings. French women are exasperated by Americans who strew evidence of their insecurities and neuroses like a cat shedding hair.

When I returned to live in the USA, each time I encountered American women I was puzzled that they competed to be the most stressed, rushed, and overwhelmed by life. American women love to see themselves as victims of forces they can't control, including forces that make them fat. French women believe themselves as capable of controlling their weight as the rest of their lives.

From French women I received much advice on hair, fashion, diet, skin care, handling men, and other pertinent subjects. I never felt these suggestions for improvement arose from bitchiness. The advice (I considered it shared wisdom) came from an attitude that we were women, and if I failed to meet the sisterhood's standards, then I should be encouraged and instructed until I was more on par with the rest. The "rest" were chic and attractive.

## MOTHERS & DAUGHTERS

French women find it easier to avoid conflict-induced excess weight because they are freer from dysfunctional relationships with their mothers. When many American women trace the source of their weight problem, they find Momma. In America, mothers too often express one of two attitudes toward their daughters. The first is competitive. The mother feels threatened by this younger female she has produced and does whatever she can to prevent her daughter from becoming attractive and successful. This grows out of a desire to control. Mothers have difficult times forcing attractive, successful daughters to do what momma wants.

Or a mother may live vicariously through her daughter. In this second case, mothers exert great pressure on their daughters to do and to be what they wanted to do and to be, but could not. Under the stress this pressure creates, daughters often turn to food for comfort. In extreme cases you get the nasty monsters anorexia and bulimia rearing their unhealthy, potentially fatal heads.

I am always touched observing French mothers with their daughters. French mothers wisely pass on to their daughters the pleasure they feel at being female. They teach these budding women skills to make them successful as women.

The difference in French mothers's attitude and American mothers's attitude results, I think, from the greater comfort French women feel with their bodies. In America, part of the Puritan legacy is that Americans don't feel comfortable with their flesh. Especially when the flesh is bare. If you have been to a French beach in the last decades you know that French women have no problem at all with bare skin.

In a poll a few years ago that asked French women if they would feel offended if asked to disrobe during a job interview, 20 percent reportedly said no.

Women uncomfortable with their bodies have little chance making their daughters feel comfortable with theirs. When someone feels uncomfortable with their body, one way of dealing with that discomfort is hiding it under layers of fat.

When they are yet children, little French girls are told by their mothers that they are beautiful; they are given instruction on how to maximize their best features. They are assured that no matter whether they are tall and willowy or short and curvaceous, they can develop their own personal style to show their body at its best and most desirable. Little French girls grow up able to take pleasure in looking and feeling attractive and to enjoy being women.

## THE LEGACY OF MADAME DE GENLIS

So why do French mothers feel obligated to pass on to their daughters the techniques to live successfully as women? The simple answer is: The French see living as an art. All art requires instruction. But there is also, I believe, an historical answer.

My theory is that French parents—particularly French mothers—feel duty-bound to teach their children the art of successful living because of the influence of an 18th century French writer and educator Madame de Genlis.

Stéphanie-Félicité Ducrest de Saint-Aubin was born in 1746 into a noble family. At 16 she was married to the Comte de Genlis and by her early twenties she, the mother of two, was a brilliant star of the French literary and political salons. She was also busy writing and publishing—and organizing educational activities for the French court. Her writings focused on her educational theories for children. She believed passionately that the most important function of adulthood was to instruct children in how to live responsibly and successfully.

In the 1770s, when she was in her thirties, Madame de Genlis was given charge of educating the Duc de Chartre's children; one of her charges became King of France. Her writings earned her international accolades. In 1785 she traveled to England where she was honored at Oxford.

Madame de Genlis had a knack for making learning interesting. Her two most important books on her educational theories were written, not as dry books of instruction, but as fiction. Madame de Genlis's *Adèle et Théodore* (published in 1782, the same year as *Les Liaisons Dangereuses*) presents her educational theories. *Les Veillées du Château* (1784) is a series of stories that show her methods in action.

One story concerns a young girl who suffers obesity-related health problems because of improper and overindulgent mothering. Delphine, undisciplined by her mother, has become a mean, tantrum-throwing little brat. Her education has been neglected. Though nine years old, she can barely read and cannot write at all. Too many sweets, no physical exercise, staying up too late for entertainments and insufficient rest have made her sick. (Delphine in 18th century France sounds unfortunately like too many children in 21st century America.)

Ellen Moers summarizes the story "Delphine" in her chapter on Madame de Genlis in her book *Literary Women*. For this book I'll shorten the tale even more. The important facts are: Delphine's mother loves her, but momma lacks the strength of character to make the effort to give her daughter a proper upbringing. When Delphine begins to suffer severe respiratory problems, the mother calls in a specialist.

The first thing the doctor does to start Delphine on the road to recovery is take her away from her mother. Not only does he move Delphine out of the house, he moves her out into the countryside to his own home and puts Delphine in the care of his wife. Little Delphine may be sick and a poor reader, but she is shrewd enough to have brought along her jewels. When she doesn't like the new regimen of nutritious food, exercise, education, and discipline, she tries to bribe her way out of it. Doesn't work.

As the months pass, under the tutelage of the doctor's wife, and influenced by the doctor's properly brought-up daughter, Delphine is transformed from a fat, sick, mean brat into a healthy, benevolent little princess.

In addition to Madame de Genlis, other French women writers have stressed the value of mothers instructing their daughters in the art of living. The 20th century French writer Colette, author of *Gigi*, devoted volumes of her writings to describing the lessons she learned from her own mother. Colette also endeared herself to women readers with those lessons for living she deftly wove through her fiction: lessons for dealing with husbands and lovers and with the difficulties of earning a living. And Colette, who, in her early fifties, took a brief sabbatical from writing to open a Parisian *institut de beauté* specializing in skin care, also slips in useful hints for looking attractive to men.

## THE TRADITION OF PERSONAL CARE

French girls grow up seeing mothers, aunts, and grandmothers taking care with their bodies and appearance. They learn by example, as well as by instruction. Since relationships between mothers and daughters are generally better in France than in the USA, French daughters won't neglect their appearance as a means of rebellion the way American daughters sometimes do.

At the first sign puberty is making changes in a French girl's skin, she is taken to an aesthetician who will analyze her skin and outline a program of care. In America, a mother will take her daughter with problem skin to a dermatologist. The approaches send different messages. In France, the message is aesthetics = beauty. In the USA, doctor = disease.

The French mother says: "You, my daughter, are being taken to this professional so that your natural features may be enhanced and you will be beautiful and happy and desired by many men."

The American girl dragged to the dermatologist gets the message she has a disease. The American message is loud and strong: SOMETHING IS WRONG WITH YOU.

The French aesthetician will prescribe a cleansing routine. Facials will begin, diet will be prescribed. The French girl will believe she has entered the pampered world of feminine beauty.

In America, the dermatologist will speak derisively about makeup and preach a sermon on the horrors of sunlight. The American girl will come away from the dermatologist thinking: Zits today and skin cancer tomorrow.

French women are more rational about ultraviolet light. They believe a tan is a way to enhance their attractiveness and get themselves to a beach or beside a pool as soon as the weather is warm enough to sit outside in a swim suit—or less.

## NON-STRESS KIDS & DOGS

French women organize their lives to avoid stress. For instance, they have not given up on the idea that children can be civilized. They hold to the notion that young, developing humans can sit at a table, eat quietly, and enjoy food. French mealtimes are pleasant without unruly, petulant children and bothersome dogs.

The French adore their dogs, pamper them, and take them everywhere, including the hairdressers and restaurants where the dogs invariably behave perfectly. As for American children, not long ago I was invited to dine with an American family who allowed their two young daughters to run and scream through the room while the meal was in progress. At the end of the main course, I realized that I had overeaten in an annoyed reaction to the children's disruption. Still, that was surely better than yielding to the temptation to yank loose the drapery cord and tie the little monsters to a chair.

## SLIM WITHOUT AEROBICS CLASS

How do French women stay slim without becoming slaves to aerobics class? How can they stay so svelte sitting around in cafés with coffee and conversation when their American sisters, to accomplish the same body shape, are pulling on their running gear and pounding out five miles?

First of all, let us remember that chic French women don't usually need to exercise to burn off fat. Moderation and practicality being the basis of the French approach to life, chic French women enjoy food, but don't overeat. They don't allow themselves to put on excess fat they must then exercise to lose. And, as I found in the 1960s—and as still seems to be the case in France today—French women get more exercise going about their daily life than women in the USA.

Many French women, I discovered, lived in apartment buildings without elevators—or in buildings in which the elevators rarely worked. The French (as all Europeans) in the 1960s were less likely than Americans to own a car. Bicycles, or feet, or public transportation were the usual means of getting around. Or one of those bouncy little mopeds: those bicycles with a little motor attached to the gears. Riding one was like riding a vibrating exercise machine.

Mopeds were always refusing to start, or conking out, or running out of petrol since they didn't have fuel gauges. The only way to check was to shake the bike and listen to the slosh. With the bike malfunctioning and running out of petrol, you spent almost as much time pushing a moped as you did riding it.

I also discovered the French got a lot of exercise on weekend hikes and on summer walking or bicycling tours. If Americans are not into such activities as much as the Europeans, climate surely plays a role. The center of France lies on the same latitude as the northernmost tip of Maine. Much of the USA is on the same latitude as the Sahara Desert. A summer walking tour of the American Plains states—or a bicycle tour of the hill country of Texas? Just thinking about it is enough to bring on dehydration and heat stroke.

Today the French are much more likely to have cars than in the 1960s. Still French women's approach to exercise hasn't changed radically since that time I was learning their secrets. A young American woman who has lived more recently in France describes it this way:

> While it's true that the French women I've known have not been exercise and aerobics-obsessed like many of my American friends, I observed that they did lead quite active lifestyles. For instance, during that standard two-hour lunch break French businesses give, my French friend and I often went water-skiing on Lake Geneve. In fact, I saw several women come down to the lake in their business suits, peel down to their swimsuits, water-ski, walk along the beach to dry off, get dressed, and return to work. I even met some French women who belonged to health clubs. The difference I noticed is that French women don't talk about exercising, they just do it.
>
> French women do much more walking in an average day than most Americans. During the week, they would walk around town to do errands, go shopping, and to visit friends. On weekends, my French friend and I were very active. We did several of the most vigorous hikes I've ever been on in my life. The women were expected to keep up with the men—and we did.
>
> In general, rather than plan (and dread!) exercise for the sake of exercising as I did at home in the U.S., in France I found myself much more active, whether it was walking around town shopping or hiking up glaciers in the Alps.

French women don't obsess about exercise. They don't talk about it. They just do it.

And hiking up an Alpine glacier at the side of an attractive Frenchman in the bracing mountain air sounds like a far more interesting way to exercise than hopping on and off a plastic step in a room full of sweaty women.

## TONED WITH MASSAGE

How do chic French women stay toned without workouts with weights or machines? They may not jog around the Luxembourg Gardens or keep one of those exercise contraptions in their apartments, but I learned they did go often for massage. A good massage can tone muscles and relieve stress. Massage gives French women a pampered, cared-for feeling. Massage provides a mental as well as a physical boost. French women believe that a good massage can break down fat on hard-to-slim spots such as thighs and around knees where exercise sometimes fails.

Unfortunately, for many years, in the USA massage had a distasteful association in the public mind with sex for hire. Fortunately, today, in the USA therapeutic massage (as opposed to massage as a cover for sex services) is becoming more available thanks to its use for sports therapy.

## NATURAL BEAUTY VS. CLEVER ILLUSION

Now the French, let us remember, are the people who invented the bra. They invented commercial hair color. In 1912 a French woman doctor began performing face lifts in Paris. I don't know whether the French invented the makeup industry, but certainly companies such as Lancôme and L'Oréal have been leaders this century.

In America "natural beauty" is more often admired than beauty created by fashion, makeup, and other aids. Natural beauty, as I use it here, could best be defined: If the fire alarm goes off at four o'clock in the morning in the hotel where you are staying and you have to go down to the lobby before you can comb your hair and makeup your face, you still look pretty good.

Anyone who read romance novels in the genre's 1980s heyday could see how prejudiced Americans are toward natural beauty. Romance novel heroines's cheeks never needed blush, their eyelashes never needed mascara, their inner thighs were always thin, and their heaving bosoms never required the assistance of a padded underwire bra. They looked perfect no matter what tattered rag they salvaged from the smoking ashes of the family mansion.

Romance novel texts were rife with sentences such as: "Sleeping, Tiara's ebony lashes drew dark accents across her perfect ivory complexion that required no camouflage of cosmetics." and "As the Count gazed at Jasmine, his heart quickened as he saw the sun burnishing the natural gold of her coppery locks that set off the exquisite emerald of her eyes."

Half the women reading those sentences went into instant states of inferiority because they knew that without a generous application of Great Lash nobody could find their eyelashes. It was only by the grace of Clairol they had any body or highlights in their limp, mouse-brown hair. And feeling inferior they reached for comfort in another piece of chocolate.

French women find this prejudice for attractiveness without cosmetic aids curious—actually counterproductive. Didn't the French philosopher Voltaire say that illusion was the source of all happiness? One does, after all, what is necessary to appear alluring.

Americans, who are fiercely competitive, find the preference for natural beauty useful. It's one more way to make the competition feel inferior. And if you shake the competition's self-confidence, you have the edge.

In America you also find, among certain groups, the idea that one's appearance is divinely ordained. I remember as a fatty growing up in the Bible Belt, pious souls told me on numerous occasions that I was overweight because it was God's will. Their attitude was that my excess weight and unattractive appearance was a damnation from which I had no recourse.

Fortunately, French women chased the notion that my fat was beyond remedy right out of my head. When I stopped overeating junk food and began to take better care of my skin, hair, and wardrobe, I might not have become a beauty, but I certainly looked better. I was no longer fat.

**PERSONAL STYLE: AN APPROACH TO LIFE**

For years I have saved a full page advertisement from an issue of the French *Elle*. Actually, the advertisement is for another French woman's magazine *Femme Pratique*, that bills itself: *Le magazine des femmes qui vont bien, merci* (The magazine for women who are doing well, thank you).

A slim young woman sits on a park bench, her bicycle leaning against the back. She is happily biting into a large *religieuse*, my favorite of the French *pâtisseries*. (A smaller cream puff atop a larger one and all this frosted with chocolate or coffee icing and set atop a round base of sweet pastry.) The caption reads: *Une femme pratique connaît ses faiblesses, c'est sa force* (An experienced woman knows her weaknesses, it's her strength).

Self-knowledge enables French women to create a personal style that goes beyond clothes. Fashion is about clothes. But personal style is about an approach to life.

Personal style is makeup, hairstyle, a signature perfume, how a woman walks, talks, gazes at the man across the table, the tone of her voice, the words she chooses, her choices in books, films, music, how she spends her time, decorates her home, cooks, how and what she eats. Personal style is interior as well as exterior. Personal style is how a French woman feels about herself.

Self-knowledge comes from careful analysis and artful effort, from beginning at an early age to decide what kind of person one is, and what kind of life one wants. Self-knowledge comes from spending long hours in front of a mirror deciding what features to emphasize, which ones require clever distraction.

American women feel great pressure to look like a popular actress or fashion icon. Though she may pick a role model and study her, a French woman does not want to look like anyone else. She wants to define her uniqueness and showcase it. No French woman is thought to be "finished" until she is at least 30. Once she develops her personal style, she sticks with it, refines it, evolves it into something splendid by mid-life. That personal style keeps her attractive for the rest of her life.

### EXAMPLES

A wonderful example of a French woman with unique personal style is Sonia Rykiel. The French fashion designer who has earned the title Queen of Knitwear dresses only in black. The inky absence of color is a dramatic counterpoint to her creamy light skin, delicate facial features, and helmet of red hair. Black only makes her tiny body look smaller and frailer. No one would ever, ever mistake Sonia Rykiel for anyone else. No one could fail to notice her when she walked into a room.

Sonia Rykiel so impressed American film director Robert Altman that he based the focus character on her in his 1994 movie *Prêt-à-Porter* (released in the USA as *Ready To Wear*). In that movie, the Sonia Rykiel character was played by Anouk Aimée who places a different spin on personal style. The French actress's trademark is her thick, silky dark hair in the cut that tousled out so memorably over the pillow in the 1966 movie classic *A Man And A Woman*. She also has a trademark gesture: running her fingers though the long strands and tossing it back.

## AMERICAN PERSONAL STYLE

Successful personal style is intentional and unapologetic. An excellent example of an American who used French principles to develop her personal style would never, ever be mistaken for a French woman.

In the early days of her career when everyone was making such a fuss about singer Dolly Parton's wigs and flashy rhinestones and flaunted D-cup style, I read a magazine article in which Dolly Parton was quoted saying: "I don't dress this way because I'm ignorant. I dress this way because I want to."

Dolly Parton explained how growing up poor in the hills she formed her own blueprint for the glamorous way she wanted to dress. Through the barrage of criticism and jokes, she never wavered from her vision. She developed a style unmistakably her own and became a superstar.

No one would ever mistake Dolly Parton for anyone else. No one could fail to notice her when she walked into a room.

## NOBODY'S PERFECT, BUT EVERYBODY'S UNIQUE

French women accept that no female is born with perfect features. Sometimes French women draw attention to one of their better features so that you neglect to notice one less attractive: hips a little broad or a chin that is a bit sharp.

The American singer Cher successfully used the distraction technique when she and Sonny Bono were performing in their weekly television show. Cher had less than perfectly aligned teeth, difficult for a singer to hide. But she also possessed an enviable flat midriff. Cher chose costumes that bared that midriff. Few people can focus at the same time on someone's navel and their teeth. Viewers, men particularly, were so busy looking at Cher's sexy figure that they didn't notice her teeth.

## LA BELLA SOPHIA

Sometimes developing a unique personal style means not hiding, but flaunting, a less than perfect feature. When international film star Sophia Loren went for her first screen tests as a teenager, she was told bluntly that she could never be a film actress.

As Sophia Loren has related in her autobiography and in interviews, film technicians told her that her nose was too long, her mouth too big, and her hips too wide for the camera. They said if she wanted to appear in movies, she must shorten her nose and lose weight. Sophia Loren said she liked her mouth and nose and hips the way they were. With a clever bit of eyelining she balanced out the mouth.

As for the nose and hips, I suspect that few males sitting in the theater and watching Sophia Loren come over the side of the boat in *Boy On A Dolphin* with that wet dress molded over her body like second skin were thinking that her nose was perhaps a bit long. Or that they saw any problem with her hips.

Sophia Loren knew what mattered and she stuck with it, as she still does in her seventies, still voluptuous and gorgeous.

## MIND CONFIDENCE

The self-confidence which keeps French women in control of their lives and their weight isn't only confidence in their bodies and personal appearance. French women have great self-confidence in their intelligence as well. An American woman who lived in France with a French family put it this way:

French women definitely felt that they were more than just ornaments by the side of men. They kept up with current events and were much more knowledgeable about history than most educated American women. They felt confident in their knowledge. They boldly spoke their opinions in the company of men.

Nancy's comments reminded me how liberated I felt when, in my first contacts with the French, I discovered that it was unnecessary for a women to play dumb in the presence of men. That had certainly been necessary in America in the 1960s when I was in college. And, unfortunately, is still necessary in today's USA in certain regions and socioeconomic groups in which men find educated, intelligent women threatening.

If French women seem better versed in history and current events than American women, it is surely due, at least in part, to the demanding French education system with its requirement for three and four hours of *devoir*, homework, each evening—even for children in the early grades. Yet academic differences aside, why do intelligent French women feel confident to let their intelligence show in mixed company? Why are French men not threatened by intelligent women who express their opinions?

For the answers to those questions we need to look back to 17th century France and an extraordinary woman, Catherine de Vivonne-Savelli, the Marquise de Rambouillet, and a type of social gathering she began: the salon.

In the early 1600s men began meeting for serious political and literary discussions. Catherine, determined that women would not be left out of these scintillating discussions, invited the finest minds of the time to her elegantly landscaped and decorated home. In this refined atmosphere, French women could participate in intellectual discussions with these leading thinkers. Other French women of charm and intelligence adopted and continued the salon tradition. In the 18th century, French salons reached their greatest brilliance. At the same period in England (which exported its social customs to America), women were separated from the men for after-dinner conversation.

Some of the women who held the French salons were beautiful and young; some were rich. Others were neither rich, nor young, nor beautiful. But they were intelligent. And their lively wits and conversation skills drew people whose goal was nothing less than finding ways to change and improve the world.

One star of 18th century Paris literary and political salons was the daughter of Louis XVI's minister of finance. Madame de Staël, born Germaine Necker, became one of the outstanding French writers of the Napoleonic period. When still a child, Germaine had participated in her mother's salon; Madame Necker's was one of the most brilliant in France during the period of the Enlightenment.

French women were given a glorious fictional role model of the brilliant, educated, accomplished talking woman. In 1807, Madame de Staël published a novel that earned her an international reputation. *Corinne* is the story of a renowned woman of genius for whom brilliant talk was her forte. The novel's high point is Corinne's coronation with the laurel wreath of genius. This sounds silly today. Yet in the early 19th century, women all over the literate world loved *Corinne*. Women writers, in particular, were inspired by the novel. Writers such as the English Jane Austen, who after more than a decade of trying, would finally publish her first novel four years after *Corinne*.

But Napoleon Bonaparte, who believed women were only to have babies and manage their households, was so upset by Madame de Staël's writing—and the ideas that it embodied—that he banished her from Paris.

Napoleon may have been a male chauvinist, but he was sufficiently intelligent to realize that manners and etiquette and social institutions such as the salon were necessary in French life. He welcomed back Madame de Récamier, the *saloniste* whom he had banished from Paris as he had Madame de Staël. Madame de Récamier was now older and in reduced financial circumstances, but with her intelligence and beauty she once again established refined salon life in Paris.

With only slight interruption, the French tradition of women demonstrating their intelligence and imagination in polite society continued. Today, thanks to the Marquise de Rambouillet and the innovations she brought to French life and to other *salonistes* who carried on her work, in France, intelligent, lively conversation on serious topics—as much as their beauty and charm—is an alluring quality for French women.

So is it any surprise that French women can stretch one bottle of mineral water or one small espresso over three hours? They are too busy debating the government's latest social policy or important new films or books to think about food or drink.

Someone should tally all the excess calories consumed by intelligent, educated American women while they sit and gag their opinions with whatever the hostess puts on the buffet table.

### LIKE WEARING A SIGNBOARD

Jane Shapiro writing in *Mademoiselle* magazine an article titled "What French Women Know" says that the way women in France dress and behave is as if they are wearing a signboard that proclaims their sensuality as well as their sexuality. The message is that they are confident, smart, witty, aware, and their poise is not merely a pose. They can be approached—if the approach is made in an intelligent manner—but adolescent or discourteous behavior will not be tolerated.

In France they say a woman such as those that Jane Shapiro describes is *bien dans sa peau*—comfortable in her skin. Personal style and a confidence in their own intelligence gives French women a secure, self-confident, in-control, comfortable-in-their-skin feeling. It provides them with a secure armor that helps them deal with pressures that often contribute to American women's feelings of insecurity, confusion, vulnerability, frustration and hopelessness. Feelings that leave American women defenseless against pressures to overeat.

An essential component of personal style is how one dresses. The way French women dress works to keep them slim.

La Mode is a means to look slim—and to be slim.

## *Praise for Chic & Slim*

*Once again, you out do your own self! Book 2 is FABULOUS! Can't wait for Book 3. Chapter after chapter, just devoured! I am not sure you know how many look up to you as a mentor of sorts, and not just the messenger. You are really an inspiration for everyone and not just people who need to lose weight. It's a mindset to get into and stay at!*
            —GIGI in CHICAGO

*I received your book and am in the process of neglecting life in general to read it. It is just Great!*
            —ANNE in ESCADA

# CHAPTER THREE

# La Mode

## NEVER UNDERESTIMATE THE POWER OF A BLACK LACE GARTER BELT

Fashion. The French. The terms are almost synonymous.

The French take the kind of interest in Paris fashion shows that Americans take in the Super Bowl.

Every day on the streets of Paris you can watch an impromptu and never-ending fashion show of alluring French women dressed in their own sensational version of chic. Not just some women. All French women you see in Paris seem possessed of a stylish elegance that somehow manages to be both refined and sexy.

Not only in Paris and on the French Riviera and at French Caribbean resorts. No matter where you find them, in France or abroad, a French woman looks more elegant, more original than anyone else.

Early in my acquaintance with French women, I learned that the way those chic women dressed and their philosophy of fashion played a major role keeping them slim. Little black dresses and lace garter belts beat the fitness studio at keeping fat off.

How exactly does this work?

**LOOKING GOOD & STAYING SLIM**

We know from scientific research, as well as common sense observation, that people who feel good about themselves are less likely to abuse food. Junk food addicts especially have wretchedly poor opinions of themselves. We also know the good feeling that comes from looking attractive is a big morale booster. How wonderful to arrive at a party and be showered with sincere positive reactions to the way we look. This praise can be a powerful amphetamine that has the same effect on curbing appetite as a chemical amphetamine.

On the other hand, to arrive at a party and believe that you are wearing the totally wrong outfit is likely to drive you to refuge in straight vodka and chips with sour cream dip. For good reason.

Our appearance makes an instant statement to others about who we are and what we are about. People who have studied the subject tell us that the most lasting impression we make on another person is the first one—the one made in the first seven seconds after someone lays eyes on us. Seven seconds! Scary when you think about it, isn't it?

So our clothes, our hair, our makeup (or lack of it), our body language, as well as our physical shape can put a relationship on a solid track or derail it before we say hello.

**MOTIVATION FOR *LA MODE***

French women dress to please men. As actress Elizabeth Taylor was once quoted as saying: "Who wants to dress to please a bunch of old broads at lunch?" Who indeed?

What is important to a French woman is that she feel good about herself and that she look good for men. Anyone with even the most minimal experience with the American male knows that he is abysmally unaware of the latest fashion trends. The only

American men likely to know the season's "in" color and style are men who aren't interested in women in the first place. American men are extremely visually oriented, yet they can rarely define what it is that makes them respond as they do. They have a poor record for noticing we are wearing a new dress or that we changed our hair color. A ten-year-old dress that fits the right way can be as seductive to the average American male as the trendiest outfit.

## LEAN CLOSETS, LEAN BODIES

When you analyze the differences in the way French and American women approach clothes, the first thing that strikes you is that American women have huge walk-in closets, rows of shelves, chests of drawers, boxes under the bed, trunks in the basement, and cedar-lined, out-of-season closets stuffed with hundreds of garments. Yet they have "nothing to wear."

French women have ten basic pieces neatly hanging in a little armoire which also accommodates their husband's suits. With these basic pieces and a few well-chosen accessories they always look perfect for any occasion. This paradox of French dressing mystifies Americans as much as the paradox of how the French eat all that rich French cuisine and have lower rates of obesity and heart disease than Americans.

French-born Véronique Vienne who frequently writes on fashion for American magazines explained the benefits of a French woman's small workable wardrobe in *Working Woman*. The piece was provocatively, if somewhat misleadingly, titled "Undressing For Success." In it, Véronique Vienne recounts how, when she arrived in the United States in 1965, she brought what seemed to her French way of thinking a perfectly elegant and adequate wardrobe: one dress, two skirts, four turtlenecks, one pearl necklace, a black patent-leather belt, two pairs of Charles Jourdan shoes, two silk scarves, an antique Piaget watch, and a

Mont Blanc pen. Her American mother-in-law, she says, found her wardrobe inadequate.

Mother-in-law marched Ms. Vienne off on a shopping trip that left her bewildered by an excess of clothes. The article makes the point that, rather than making dressing easier, having an excess makes deciding what to wear more difficult and stressful.

So, practical as it is, time-saving as it is, recommended in thousands of American women's magazine articles as it has been, why don't more American women maintain a small, functional wardrobe and make deciding what to wear easier?

First, small functional wardrobes go against the basic American belief that more is always better. (Remember, in America, too much is never enough.) Second, American women don't feel comfortable, as French women do, finding one or two outfits that make them look wonderful and wearing them for a variety of occasions. Perhaps for good reason. I speak from experience.

**SAD BUT TRUE STORY**

When I returned to the U.S. in the early 1980s, I was very much into the French system of dressing. In a shop I found (on sale, no less) a wonderfully practical go-everywhere dress. A dress which was extremely flattering to me. Everyone complimented me on it—even elderly men and small children. That autumn I probably wore that dress at least part of four days a week. One day I ran into a friend of my mother's at a meeting. "You're always wearing that dress," she said. "Now which airline do you work for?"

**FRENCH FASHION LESSON**

That experience has not deterred me. Years ago, a French acquaintance convinced me one well-chosen, flattering outfit could go anywhere day after day with an assortment of accessories. She returned from a shopping trip to Paris with a classically cut wool skirt and cashmere sweater in the season's featured color. Trimly belted at the waist, the outfit simply screamed Paris chic. The skirt and sweater drew compliments at a dinner party and a few days later at a luncheon. She wore it shopping and to drive the kids to school.

I couldn't understand. To my American way of thinking, you couldn't be seen day after day in the same clothes. Then I thought about it.

What's the point of dressing? You want to look attractive, you want to be comfortable, you want to feel good about yourself. If you had one outfit that met those criteria and made you appear more fashionable than anyone else, why not wear it? Again and again and again.

But one spring morning I thought the French woman had taken that beautiful outfit too far. My young son and I were walking the dog on the beach behind our house when she came down with a neighbor to bring the children to play. The other woman, another American, and I were dressed in casual pants and shirts; the French woman was wearing her new Parisian outfit. Horrified the sand would ruin her beautiful skirt, I offered to go back to my house and bring a towel for her to sit on.

My French friend told me, *"Non, merci,"* in that firm but bemused way in which the French refuse offers from Americans for things they consider totally unnecessary. She untied the scarf around her neck, spread it on the sand and arranged herself on it. Two hours later when she left, the skirt was still spotless. The scarf, no doubt, was easily revived by a brief visit to soapsuds.

Compared with the French woman's Parisian chic, the other American woman and I in our casual attire looked like provincial bumpkins.

## TRAVELING LIGHT

I always marveled at how unencumbered the French managed to come to the beach. During the swimming season, time after time, they arrived without a towel and wearing their swimsuit under their clothes. After an invigorating swim, they walked briskly up and down the long beach until their swimsuit dried in the sea breeze. They put their clothes back on over their swimsuit and left. How convenient, I thought.

Even though the Mediterranean was right outside our back gate, thinking American, I couldn't imagine going down to the beach without, at very minimum: towels, sandals, beach cover-up, books, suntan lotion, and mineral water. And you may have realized as you read, a swim in the waves followed by a 45-minute walk burned up a lot more calories than lolling on a beach towel sipping cold drinks and snacking.

## POOL FASHION

Even convinced as I was that French women had a workable system to keep them slim, sometimes the extremes to which they took a small multipurpose wardrobe seemed almost loony. At hotels I saw French women come down to the pool wearing their swimsuits with exactly the same high heels that they had worn from the airport. Totally crazy, I thought. With a swimsuit you wore flat-heeled shoes, preferably something that provided traction on the wet tiles around the pool.

Then I remembered French women generally aren't tall; they wear high heels because those shoes make their legs look longer and slimmer. I asked myself, "Did you ever see Miss America walk down the runway in shower thongs?"

French women know what they are doing. Which brings up another chief difference in the way American and French women approach fashion.

**FUN & GAMES VS. AGONY & STRESS**

For French women, fashion is *un jeu*, a game to be played and enjoyed. Unfortunately, for too many American women, dressing themselves is a stress-generating struggle to accommodate lifestyle needs with numerous and always-changing fashion dos and don'ts—and keep it all within budget and within time available for shopping.

The cartoon Cathy in the fitting room trying on the clothing industry's latest offering, looking in the mirror, and screaming "AIIIIGGGGHHHHH!!" is often the American woman's fashion experience. For too many American women, as for Cathy, fitting room frustration sends them running for solace in food. Straight out of the dress boutique and into the ice cream shop.

In a *Dallas Morning News* interview with cartoon Cathy's creator Cathy Guisewite, in almost every paragraph of this article by Valli Herman, I was reminded of major differences between French and American women's approach to fashion and how these different attitudes make crucial differences in weight control.

Though Cathy Guisewite is now trim and petite, she says she gained 50 pounds in college. This explains, I think, her success at drawing strips about the cartoon Cathy's perennial struggles with overeating with which American women identify so strongly.

When I read that Cathy Guisewite told her interviewer that she thinks fashion is a microcosm for the overwhelming choices American women must cope with today, I thought of the ways French women have of simplifying those choices today's living demands. Ms. Guisewite bemoaned women's extra expectations and the difficulty of trying to live up to 15 different images and having the proper outfit for each.

A personal style simplifies life for French women. A French woman doesn't feel pressured to come up with 15 different images. She has perfected one image: her own personal and unique image and she showcases it everywhere everyday.

A French woman avoids the what-will-everyone-else-be-wearing? dilemma. It doesn't matter. She wears what she feels will make her look her best no matter what the occasion. Personal style and classic dressing serve French women well.

I was reminded of this watching a segment of CNN's "Style." The host Elsa Klensch had just reviewed a Paris fashion show by one of the leading designers in which 9-foot tall, 99-pound models (I'm exaggerating, but not much) had slouched and pouted down the runway in bottom-hugging skirts in the waif babydoll look.

The show then cut to an interview with a French woman who was spokeswoman for a quality line of French shoes. The woman wore classic French style: slim black skirt, black silky blouse, black blazer with a jewel bright scarf in the jacket pocket. Her hairstyle was the one we've been seeing on French women since we first spotted Leslie Caron with her face-framing cap of short dark curls in *An American In Paris* in 1951.

Fashion on the runway is designed to provoke the attention of the fashion media who grow more jaded every year. Runway fashion is theater. Often very entertaining theater.

A French woman's personal style will usually be quite different than what we see in the media photos of the Paris fashion shows.

**THE PERFECT FIT**

In the history of weight control in America, when American women stopped relying on dressmakers and began buying ready-to-wear in industry-prescribed sizes, their problem with fat escalated. The connection is easy to see. How depressing when the size 8 pulls at the hips and you have to buy a size 10. Your subconscious comes into play and begins to broadcast the message: *You are a size 10.* Soon, unfortunately, your body conforms to what your mind tells it. You gain weight until you are a size 10.

French women often avoid the depressing business of sizes by sewing for themselves or having a dressmaker who can whip up a copy of the latest couture creation from a magazine photograph at a fraction of the cost.

Many of these talented dressmakers learned their craft in the big name fashion houses of Paris in menial—and not-so-menial jobs. The dressmaker who sewed for me had accompanied her husband to Paris to attend dental school. While her husband studied dentistry, she apprenticed as a *petite-main* in one of the name fashion houses. By the time her husband completed his training in the pulling and filling of teeth, she had learned the techniques of cutting, sewing, and fitting women's clothes.

From my experience with Madame La Couturière, I learned how the cut and fit of clothes keeps those chic French women slim.

My friend who recommended the dressmaker warned me before I made my first appointment, "She fits the clothes to you exactly. If you gain a pound, you won't be able to wear the dress." And that's the way French women want their clothes. They want them body-hugging, just short of too snug. This fit shows the feminine form at its most seductive. (Remember Brigitte Bardot is those sheaths.)

The question of size never comes up with a dressmaker. They simply cut and fit the outfit to your body. And they do it in a way that is the most flattering to your figure.

Perfect fit is another advantage of having a well-trained dressmaker rather than buying off-the-rack. "When you come for your first fitting," Madame La Couturière lectured me, "you will wear the exact lingerie and the exact shoes you plan to wear with the dress." From Madame I learned a lesson I find useful even when I shop for ready-to-wear.

No doubt closets in the USA would contain fewer unworn clothes if, before they handed over the plastic, American women tried on the prospective purchase with the undergarments and accessories they plan to wear with the outfit. That disastrous line too often uttered by sales personnel on commission: "Oh, that dress will look just fine once you get your control-top panty hose on." Well, maybe.

One more benefit that French women reap from those body-tailored fashions they favor is that those clothes demand that you stand and sit straight. They are sufficiently tight that slumped shoulders or an unrestrained abdomen are instantly noticed; they make you look like a tired turtle. And French women's impeccable posture is just one of numerous tricks they use to make themselves appear slimmer than they really are.

## NO SLOPPY OLD SWEAT SUITS

Their more formal manner of dressing also helps chic French women control their weight. French women wear dresses and skirts more often than American women. These, after all, are the women who put on makeup and high heels on Saturday morning just to go to the butcher shop. Especially in cities, even if French women wear jeans or casual clothes, they wear those clothes in a finished, well-pressed, accessorized, dressed-up manner.

Formal dressing works against overeating. When you look like the cover of *Harper's Bazaar*, are you going to sit around gorging on greasy pizza and guzzling colas?

On the other hand, sloppy old clothes seem an invitation to sprawl back and stuff yourself with everything in the refrigerator.

## NEVER UNDERESTIMATE THE POWER
## OF A BLACK LACE GARTER BELT

Even French women's lingerie helps to keep them slim. French women believe what they wear underneath their clothes is as important, perhaps more important, than the clothes themselves. Silky, sexy, feminine lingerie makes French women feel feminine and desirable.

So what does your underwear have to do with how much you weigh?

When I was fat (but constantly dieting), I did a lot of overeating at times I temporarily forgot my previous resolve to let real hunger, rather than my eyes, dictate the amount I ate. For French women, pretty silky lingerie is a next-to-the-skin constant reminder to make the choices that pay off in slimness. Their belief in this principle is demonstrated by the fact that there are almost as many lingerie shops in Paris as bakeries.

In *Roman Holiday*, the movie that won Audrey Hepburn an Academy Award for best actress, Audrey Hepburn as the European princess complains she hates her underwear. Her lady-in-waiting reminds Her Highness that she has very nice underwear. The princess says yes it is nice underwear—for someone 200-years-old.

Even though in 1952 nobody saw a princess's underwear, the princess knew that her lingerie made a difference in how she felt about herself. (Today, the media show us more of princesses than we bargained for. Alas.)

Audrey Hepburn was an actress who was naturally slim. With assistance from Givenchy, she made tall, slim, and elegant her own personal style during the same years Sophia Loren beguiled audiences with her voluptuousness. A few decades ago, we accepted a variety of body shapes as beautiful. Today, too often, beauty means everyone must fit the same emaciated mold. And the mold is getting skinnier every day.

## PERFUME, THE SECRET WEAPON

The French may not have invented perfume. But French perfumers such as Guerlain, Lanvin, Patou, and Caron have developed many of the best known and most widely-used scents in the world. Early in the 20th century French fashion designers began designing perfumes as well as clothing.

A woman might not be able to afford a Chanel, a Dior, or a Givenchy dress. But she can buy (or receive as a gift) one of the couture designers' perfumes. Wearing the scent makes her feel as elegant as if she were wearing the designer's dress.

For a French woman, fragrance is a potent weapon in her personal style arsenal. She feels undressed without it. Choosing her fragrance is serious business. She selects a scent that best expresses her personality and wears it, as Coco Chanel told us, as her personal signature. It as necessary to her feeling of being well-dressed as her shoes or hair style.

One writer explained in a French fashion magazine article that fragrance was necessary for *"l'amour, la patience, le génie, l'imagination."* For love, patience, genius, and imagination.

For a French woman, fragrance is a magic potion she uses to weave men under her spell. A spell to which a French male gladly submits.

French perfumes are expensive, an extravagance, but an extravagance that makes a chic French woman feel wonderful and special. She feels she is worth the price that perfume cost. And when you believe you are special, are you going to stuff yourself with starchy, greasy food that will make you fat and unattractive?

**FRENCH GOLDEN RULE OF CHIC : Keep It Simple**

Simple means building your wardrobe around a neutral color such as black, brown, navy, or gray. Adding the "in" color of the season with an accessory. Simple is also solid colors for your winter wools and a tiny print for your summer cottons.

Simple is tailored, classic clothes with simple lines such as Jacqueline Kennedy Onassis's favored A-line.

Simple is plain leather pumps and one quality hand bag that lasts for years.

Simple is having clothes that fit perfectly so you don't have to keep checking if they are gaping open, riding up, pulling out, sagging down or spontaneously performing any rearrangement that will detract from your appearance.

Simple is staying slim so you can make your investment in classic, quality clothes pay off for years and years.

Simple is keeping jewelry to a minimum: your wedding ring or one antique ring, a good watch, earrings in real gold or silver. Or it's bare hands and ears and real pearls (or good quality fakes) that you wear with everything—even with your cotton work shirt, as I saw in a magazine photograph of a French potter.

Simple is short, perfectly filed nails without polish to chip and look tacky when you don't have time for touch-up.

Simple is an attractive face through healthy eating and drinking and a program of skin care, rather than trying to cover up blemishes with heavy foundations and concealers that can streak, rub off on men's shirts, or gum up your pores.

Simple is a well-cut, low-maintenance, indestructible by wind and rain hairstyle. Short, if you have that natural curl in your hair as many French women do. Longer, so it can be twisted up into a French twist or chignon if your hair is naturally straight.

Simple is not depending on clothes and accessories to make you look attractive, but rather letting your aura of self-confidence, the way you walk and sit, the intelligent and amusing things you say, the sparkle in your eyes, the tone of your voice, and the alluring scent of your perfume make you attractive whether you are wearing a sweater and jeans from the flea market or an evening dress from a designer collection.

Simple is *très chic.*

## EVERY DAY CHICER & CHICER

I always assumed the practice of using affirmations, positive statements to change our feelings and actions, was the invention of some California New Age guru meditating in a hot tub somewhere out in the further reaches of Marin County.

But the technique is credited to a French psycho-therapist Émile Coué. He believed repeating a positive phrase in a confident voice when the mind was receptive would fix the idea in the subconscious and override negative beliefs.

Coué instructed patients to repeat "Every day in every way, I am becoming better and better." Twenty times, three sessions a day. French women are still putting Coué's system into practice. Whatever a French woman is wearing, she will tell herself that she looks attractive. She convinces herself. And believing, she convinces everyone who sees her. American women put themselves in conflict with fashion. The result of this conflict is frustration. Consequently, American women fail to use *la mode* to keep them slim as French women do.

Ultimately, of course, not only the way you dress, but also what foods you eat will make the difference in whether you are chic and slim or frumpy and dumpy. Here is the paradox that amazes Americans: French cuisine keeps French women slim. Really.

# CHAPTER FOUR

# La Cuisine

## FOIE GRAS & MOUSSE AU CHOCOLATE KEEP YOU SLIMMER THAN LOW-FAT & SUGARLESS

Not since the French writer Colette created Gigi did fiction give us as delightful a French female as Nicole Bouvier.

This slim, beautiful, chicly dressed *Parisienne* in author Peter Mayle's *Hotel Pastis: A Novel of Provence* is an appealing composite of all those chic French women I studied so diligently.

Mayle's protagonist, the British advertising executive Simon Shaw, can't help comparing the French Nicole to his British former wife Caroline. Both women are slim and beautiful. But their attitudes toward food are strikingly different. For Caroline eating is an exercise in pushing a salad around on her plate. But Nicole, Simon notes, has a hearty appetite for the meals they share. He observes how she eats "plenty of bread." She enjoys her wine and champagne and red meat. And when Simon comments to her on her eating, Nicole says she eats like a *routier*, a truck driver.

Wouldn't that be wonderful: To be as chic and slim as those oh-so attractive *Parisiennes* and still pack in food like a truck driver?

Numerous American weight control methods work. All have their special gimmick, but most share prohibitions against sugars, red meat, fats, and white flour products. The plans demand vigorous exercise a certain number of minutes per day. The promise is that if you follow the plan, you will be slim as the skinniest Hollywood starlet. I have nothing but admiration for women who follow one of these methods. I just can't live that way.

That's why I prefer the French system. I enjoy many foods that those diet programs regularly prohibit. High fat cheese, for instance. I am not sufficiently masochistic to run five miles a day or work out at a fitness center. Who wants to spend time in a place that smells like an old wet dog on a hot day?

## EATING FRENCH

*Haute cuisine, cuisine régionale, cuisine bonne maman, cuisine bourgeoise, nouvelle cuisine, cuisine minceur.* What is the real French cuisine?

When I met chic French women, *nouvelle cuisine* was yet to be invented. Thank goodness. I understand that the French who actually tried to eat the stuff have now gone back to the good old *cuisine bourgeoise*, those tasty, well-flavored, meat and vegetable dishes that made the American writer Ernest Hemingway claim that Paris was a moveable feast. Many French never tried *nouvelle cuisine*. They left minute portions of meat and vegetables with strange flavorings hand-arranged on a plate to the tourists.

As for *cuisine minceur* (slimming cuisine), Chef Michel Guérard is credited with creating this lowered fat version of French cuisine. The French believe that, even if you are reducing calories in a dish, the food should taste and look marvelous.

So what is real French cuisine? When I was so intensely studying those chic French women, they were eating traditional French cuisine, much the same as that served in a French bistro: chicken roasted with vegetables, grilled sausages, vegetables *au beurre*, heavenly mousses, and lots of good French onion soup.

The French revere good food and give dishes lyrical names such as *Foie de veau à la Lyonnaise* (liver and onions), *Salade d'haricots blancs frais aux olives* (bean salad), *Rougets à la Bonifacienne* (baked fish), *Fraginat de boeuf à la Catalane* (stew). In the USA, foods are christened with names like Big Mac, The Whopper, and All You Can Eat Special. All carry the message of a large portion. When the French dine, they seek the gastronomic equivalent of listening to a symphony. Americans whose musical tastes lean toward strum, bang, and twang aren't as concerned with the flavor of the food as whether there is a lot of it.

On the following pages are the chief differences in the way I ate when I was fat—and perennially dieting—and the way the French eat and stay slim.

**REAL BUTTER**

The French consumption of real 100 percent animal fat butter mystifies Americans so piously eating their low-fat and no-cholesterol vegetable oil spreads. The French use butter extensively in their cuisine. But keep in mind two things. First, butter is expensive in France. Second, the French are thrifty. The French housewife will not use more butter in a dish than absolutely necessary. Consider, too, that the French who eat bread with every meal don't butter it. With one major exception: the small amount they spread on their breakfast roll or *tartine*. And have you ever watched a French woman spread butter? First they take this tiny bit of butter on the tip of their knife; then, they spread and spread and spread. Watching the process makes me think some law said that every air space in the surface of the bread must have the equal micro-amount of butter.

The French don't eat margarine. If you have no firsthand experience with the French, I cannot explain to you the total contempt and disdain in which the French hold this butter substitute. The irony here is that they invented the stuff. Back in the late 1860s a French chemist Mège-Mouriès concocted the original version primarily out of animal fats. The early margarines must have been vile: in Europe, whale oil was frequently a component.

Today Americans, convinced that margarine is healthier than real butter (though the medical community raised questions about margarine's trans-fatty acids), spread vegetable oil margarine liberally over their bread; the French use real animal fat butter sparingly.

## OUT, OUT DAMN FAT

True, the French love their steak and "French" fried potatoes. But in many French meat and vegetable dishes, at some stage in the preparation, the fat is totally removed. Too, baking, roasting, poaching, and grilling (where all the fat falls down into the fire) are used frequently for preparing meat, chicken, and fish. Before I began to "eat French," I had usually eaten fish fried, frequently in batter. Adjusting to poached fish took years. And I still prefer fish cooked other ways than in water. I generally opt for baked fish, well seasoned with herbs and sprinkled with fresh lemon juice. An enormous reduction in fat from fried versions of fish.

The French avoid canned soups. But in making those stocks on which many French soups are based—whether chicken, beef, or fish—a point comes in the preparation where the soup stock is made fat-free. The French, it seems to me, have rather laborious methods for this procedure. For Americans whose refrigerators are generally larger than those of the French, it's easiest to chill the stock to solidify the fat; then, lift it off.

Another area in which the French eat minimal fat where Americans consume much is in salad dressing. The French salad, if served dressed, invariably comes tossed at the last moment in a vinaigrette. The variations are many and individual, but basically you begin with a good quality oil, usually olive, into which you whisk various spices and a wine vinegar. Depending on the greens you plan to dress, the proportions range from four parts oil to one part vinegar to half and half. In areas with good citrus, lemon or lime juice is substituted for part or all of the vinegar. Often a cruet of oil and another of vinegar are placed on the table and you sprinkle these over your salad greens.

The French also avoid extra calories on sandwiches by spreading their bread lightly with butter or (in the South) olive oil—or with one of their world-famous Dijon mustards. For decades weight control advisers have been telling Americans to substitute mustard for mayonnaise, or for the equally fatty vegetable oil-based mayonnaise look-alike sold as "salad dressing." Still many Americans maintain their devotion to the creamy white spread. "Because it tastes so good with sliced white bread," explained one of my friends.

## FRENCH BREAD

Only the French could turn bread into an aid to weight control. French bread by law is flour, water, yeast, and salt. Nothing more. Nothing less. It provides a low-fat, complex carbohydrate food.

The long, thin crusty baguette is as much a symbol of France as the Eiffel Tower. Yet the baguette is not traditional French bread. Like that other well-known French bakery item, the croissant—which the French consider pastry, not bread—it's an import. An Austrian diplomat in Paris introduced the long thin Viennese-style loaf in the mid-19th century. Especially in the cities, the more elegant bread took over the place previously held by the whole wheat sourdough loaf that had fed the French for centuries.

As for the croissant, Marie Antoinette brought the recipe when she came from her native Austria to marry King Louis XVI. And she, history claims, added her own spark to the fire of the French

Revolution by saying of the populace demanding bread, "Let them eat cake." Actually it would make a tidier anecdote if she had said, "Let them eat croissants." In any case Marie Antoinette lost her head on the guillotine. The French monarchy perished; the croissant survived.

As for revolution, the French underwent another 200 years after the original. This time the revolution was in bread. Parisian baker Lionel Poilâne waged an energetic campaign to bring the French back to the more nutritious traditional *boule*, a round whole wheat sourdough loaf.

Poilâne's efforts rated him attention by the international media, including a cover story in *Smithsonian* magazine. His method makes country bread by an ingenious marriage of traditional techniques and modern technology in which quality has not been sacrificed. Poilâne bread became immensely popular. For a bread that will help those chic French women eat rich French cuisine and still stay slim, this all-natural bread made with stone-ground flour beats the more popular white flour baguette.

Alas, somewhere in the beginning of the 20th century, America went off the track as far as bread is concerned. American factory-produced, plastic-packaged, squishy, anemic pseudo-bread is the worst bread on the planet.

American bread contains sugars, fats, and chemicals. A friend's loaf of bread listed the following ingredients: wheat flour, malted barley flour, niacin, iron, thiamin, mononitrate riboflavin, water, soy fiber, wheat gluten, corn syrup, yeast, wheat bran, molasses, honey, salt, whey, sodium stearoyl lactylate, calcium stearoyl-2-lactylate, monoglycerides, ethoxylated mono and diglycerides, calcium iodate, polysorbate 60, calcium peroxide, guar gum, vinegar, calcium sulfate, ferrous sulfate, thiamin hydrochloride, monocalcium phosphate, and ammonium sulfate. Oh, dear!

Perhaps because of all the chemicals, American "factory" bread lacks that yeasty taste, hearty texture, and wonderful aroma that makes freshly baked bread like eating heaven. Small wonder Americans spread this pseudo-bread with so much fat and sugar.

"French bread" is sold in America, but, unfortunately, most bread labeled French bread resembles bread baked in France to about the same degree most American women resemble Catherine Deneuve or Audrey Tautou.

I didn't like American bread even when I didn't know any other sort existed. Growing up in the United States, the only bread I knew was sliced, packaged store bread. I thought it tasted like an old bathroom sponge. The only "cheese" served at our table was a cheese product easily mistaken for edible plastic. At age eight I read the children's story *Heidi*. At the description of Heidi and her grandfather eating a supper consisting solely of bread and cheese, I burst into tears. I cried to think all that poor little girl and her elderly grandfather had to eat was Wonder Bread and Velveeta.

But things are looking up in the bread department in the USA. With a little effort, you find reasonably good quality artisan bread in bakeries and supermarkets. Bread machines make at-home baking of quality breads easy. Many mixers and food processors also have a dough hook that eliminates mixing and kneading.

### *À VOTRE SANTE!* WINE FOR WEIGHT LOSS

Initially I thought chic French women drank much more wine than they do. Actually, average annual consumption of wine in France works out to about 73 liters per person. That is one small three and a half ounce portion with lunch and another with the evening meal. Each portion measures less than a half cup. And men drink more than women.

Compare that with the annual American soft drink consumption as reported by the Beverage Marketing Corporation at 556 cans (12 oz. size) per year. The University of California at Berkeley Wellness Letter people did some mathematics and came up with a figure of 83,400 calories for those 556 cans. If the average American woman needs about 2000 calories per day for normal weight, those 83,400 calories are equal to the entire caloric needs for 41 days, or almost six weeks.

## MINERAL WATER

Another surprise was that the French are as serious about their *eaux minérales* as about their *vins*. The French will as readily discuss mineral waters as wine vintages. French women will tell you which among the dozens of brands of bottled mineral waters that they believe are best for weight control. They will advise drinking mineral water for beautiful skin.

At first, when I saw those very slim, very chic French women sitting at a sidewalk cafe sipping a Perrier with a slice of lemon, I felt a mixture of anger and envy. How could they prefer to drink plain water? I wondered. Yet rationally I understood that not only was mineral water free from all that sugar in the cola drinks to which I was so addicted, but the bottled water came from pure natural spring sources high in the mountains. The water contained important and healthy minerals. Americans have become larger consumers of bottled water in the past few years. Yet when I heard it referred to as "designer water," I feared that once more Americans had missed the point. My friends, mineral water has definite health benefits—*if* it's from a good proven source.

Note here that, because bread and wine are a regular part of almost every French meal, if a chic French women finds one of her form-fitting fashions becoming snug, she cuts back on bread for a couple of days and replaces the mealtime wine with mineral water. That often takes care of the problem.

One American did not miss the point about mineral water. In an article in *Family Circle* magazine, country music singer Reba McEntire credited much of her success losing 25 pounds in the 1980s to switching from beer to mineral water.

Often the way to slim does not require signing up for an expensive weight control program, nor buying an expensive piece of workout equipment. Rather you need to pinpoint what is adding a substantial number of calories to your daily intake—such as the beer in Reba McEntire's case. Changing that one thing can mean you can leave almost everything else the same. No major behavioral modifications needed.

### ICED TEA? *NON, MERCI*

One beverage hardly any French person drinks, but which I guzzled continually when I was fat, is iced tea. I grew up in a region where we drank iced tea the year round with every meal except breakfast. Ten inches of snow could be blanketing the wheat fields and we would still be getting those ice cubes out of the refrigerator and pouring the tea over them. I mistakenly believed that, drunk without sugar, iced tea was a "diet beverage." Now I know that iced tea poses hindrances to weight loss.

Iced tea glasses are huge, holding about twice as much as the average water glass. On a hot day (and we had a lot of them where I grew up), I might slosh down two glasses per meal and several in between. That is a *lot* of caffeine and tannic acid. Nutritionists warn that tannic acid interferes with iron absorption. Not enough iron and we feel exhausted. And if we feel exhausted, we aren't going to be moving around burning up calories, are we? We might just grab a quick sugar boost from a candy bar.

Excess caffeine, besides depleting us of the B vitamins and vitamin C, can increase appetite and induce a craving for sweets. (Maybe that's why in my iced tea drinking days I couldn't pass the cookie jar without taking one.) Unfortunately no-calorie iced tea can cause you to take in more calories in the long run—or suffer uncomfortable hunger pangs. The French stick with their mineral water with a squeeze of lemon as a hot weather thirst quencher.

### *APÉRITIFS OUI,* COCKTAILS NO

In the beverage department, the French save calories with their pre-meal drink of preference, the *apéritif.* Many of these drinks are bitter. Others are very bitter.

At first I thought the French were crazy to drink an *apéritif* such as Pernod instead of better-tasting mixed drinks. Then I realized how drinking *apéritifs* worked to keep them slim. The French frown on excessive alcohol consumption because they believe it interferes with enjoying well-prepared food. Alcohol can also cause you to forget those good intentions to eat moderately. It can cause you to do other foolish—and often un-chic—things.

So if the drink in your glass tastes like an unfortunate blend of furniture polish and boiled weeds, are you going to toss back three in the hour before dinner?

No, you are going to do what the French do: sip one of those tiny glasses of *pastis* or Campari for hours.

### *ESCARGOTS* & OTHER CRITTERS

The same principle that regulates French alcohol consumption keeps the French eating moderately. Many French dishes don't taste instantly gratifying the way American dishes do. It requires a sophisticated palate to appreciate their taste. And let's face it, our Gallic friends eat a lot of weird stuff that Americans don't even want to discuss at the table, much less to find on their plates. Would you really want a second helping of cow's stomach? Or snails? The French swallow two billion of those slimy little critters each year. Two billion snails! Think about it.

## THE BIGGEST DIFFERENCE: FRUITS & VEGGIES

The biggest difference in the way I ate as a fatty and the way chic French women eat is: the amount of fresh fruits and vegetables.

Chic French women eat a lot of fresh fruits and vegetables; as a fatty, I ate little. For several good reasons. Foremost was that the quality of fruit and vegetable dishes available to me never approached the excellence of the array of homemade cakes, pies, and cookies always there to tempt me.

The 1950s in America was the heyday of commercially canned fruits and vegetables: poor substitutes for the taste of fresh. Also the quality of produce in our little grocery then was abysmal; the selection limited.

Quality and selection of produce have improved in recent years in the USA, though most produce is shipped semi-green and you have to ripen it at home. My biggest current complaint about American supermarket fruits and vegetables is the damage done in-store by shoppers who squeeze (thus bruise) in a misguided belief this is a test for quality.

Years ago television commercials brainwashed people to squeeze bathroom tissue; now some think what is good for toilet paper is good for tomatoes. The French are more intelligent shoppers. In France the vendor likely also grew and harvested the produce. Bruising his merchandise would be like abusing his children.

Unfortunately, most vegetables served today in all but the most upscale American eating establishments are tasteless and overcooked. Frequently smothered by some starchy, greasy substance masquerading as a sauce. Restaurants in which you can order a piece of fresh fruit are rare. With Americans eating so many meals outside the home, no wonder the national consumption of vegetables and fruits is low—while the readings on bathroom scales are high.

## ALL THAT *FROMAGE*

The regular consumption of *fromage*, cheese—much of it very high fat cheese—is more of the French Paradox that so mystifies Americans. How can the French eat cheese such as Brie (60 percent fat and proudly proclaims so on the label) twice a day and avoid obesity and heart attacks?

From my experience observing chic French women, I believe the answer is: they never eat very much cheese at any one time. The meal progresses from an hors d'oeuvre, to meat and vegetable, to salad. Next comes the cheese tray. Your average French person cuts off this small sliver of cheese that they carefully spread on more French bread. If you want cheese, why not eat a quarter pound of Brie and come back for seconds?

Because in the French system one eats a small amount of cheese with bread in the course following (sometimes with) the salad course. Moderation is the watchword, remember? So the French are able to eat wonderful Camembert, or a Roquefort— or another of their 250 (or is it 450?) kinds of cheese—yet avoid those terrible things the Nouveaux Puritans assure us will happen if we eat any cheese, other than non-fat cottage cheese.

## SUGAR, MY SWEET

At the time of the first publication of this book in 1997, the per capita sugar consumption in France was about five pounds per person per year. Indications are, however, that French per capita consumption might be even *less* today. In the USA, average per capita sugar consumption is usually given as 140 to 150 pounds per person per year. Then, there is all that high fructose corn syrup that seems to be added to an endless number of processed foods, and especially to sweetened soft drinks, baked desserts, jams and jellies.

How can French sugar consumption be so low when they eat all those scrumptious pastries? First, real French pastry is not as high in refined sugar as you might think. Traditional versions use much fruits, nuts, and whipped egg whites. French pastries are small. What you find sold in the USA as French pastry is often a larger, Americanized version with less fresh fruit, egg whites, real cream, and nuts—and with far more oils, refined sugar, white flour, fillers, and chemical preservatives. If the French thought a pastry chef had added carrageenan, a filler often used in American "French" pastry, they would dust off the guillotine.

Fresh fruit, not dessert, ends a typical French meal. Even when the French serve flan or a sorbet, even a chocolate mousse, the portions are small. (I mean *très petite*.)

Economics plays a role here. Before I left the United States I was told that French sugar was more expensive than that sold in America and that I would not be baking cakes, pies, and cookies the way I had in the United States. I didn't.

Traditionally in France, pastries are bought to serve as dessert with Sunday dinner. We think of the custom of afternoon tea as English, but the French are also enthusiastic tea sippers. French pastries often accompany the tea.

Yet, whenever the French eat pastries, they invariably eat them seated and with ceremony. No chic French woman keeps a stash of Oreos in her desk to give her an afternoon energy boost. Remember, you hardly need an energy boost mid-afternoon if you spent two hours mid-day eating a three-course lunch that included ample protein and complex carbohydrates.

The French avoid consuming hidden sugar the way Americans do. They eat little processed food, the source of much sugar Americans eat unaware. Americans eat tons of sugar in commercial sauces and condiments (ketchup and salad dressing, for example), in breads, and certainly in carbonated soft drinks.

## TELL ME WHAT YOU EAT

*"Tell me what you eat, and I will tell you what you are."* Often a food discussion includes that quote from the French gastronomy expert Brillat-Savarin.

Anthelme Brillat-Savarin was not a chef, he was a lawyer and politician with great interest in food. During the Terror following the French Revolution, he spent three years in exile in the United States. After Brillat-Savarin returned to France from America, he wrote the classic work on the art and science of good eating *La Physiologie du Goût* (The Physiology of Taste) in which that much-quoted aphorism appeared. I like to think that Brillat-Savarin's exile in America gave him perspectives on food that inspired the work considered some of the best gastronomy writing of all time.

*"Tell me what you eat, and I will tell you what you are."*

The paradox is that the French eat fat: butter, cream, red meats, and eggs, yet they struggle less with excess body fat than Americans who eat products labeled "low-fat" and "no-fat." Perhaps if Brillat-Savarin had come to America in 1994 instead of 1794, he would have said, *"Tell me what you do not eat, and I will tell you what you are not."*

If you do *not* eat a lot of American processed pseudo-food, you are *not* fat.

The foods French women eat, as much as the foods they do not eat, keep them slim. And the way they set up their households and shop also works to make them slim.

# CHAPTER FIVE

# Le Shopping & La Déco

## BOULANGERIES, BOUDOIRS & BIDETS

It's amazing when you think about it.

French women weren't given the vote until 1946, almost three decades after American women won that right. The women's liberation movement hardly exists in France. Yet French women have cleverly managed to arrange their lives in ways that free them from household drudgery better than their nominally more liberated American sisters. Even when Americans have long had bigger and better equipped homes, supermarkets, more household appliances, and shopping centers larger than some French villages.

As a nice little bonus, the way French women organize their households and shop helps keep them slim.

Unfortunately, the downside of American superiority in household convenience and shopping is that a greater percentage of American women are overweight.

Ah, you say. You knew your sister-in-law should never have given you that handheld blender for Christmas.

Sorry. It's more complicated than that.

### LE SHOPPING

Consider food shopping. Most French women shop daily or every two or three days. They buy only what the family will eat in that time. And they have a very sure sense of exactly how much the family will eat. Leftovers, *restes* are considered evidence of inefficient housekeeping. As the French food bible *Larousse Gastronomique* primly explains, a large quantity of leftovers is evidence of careless planning on the part of the cook, or of poorly prepared food. Oh, my!

If you buy only what fits into your shopping bag, and if you plan carefully so you don't prepare more food than will be eaten at a meal, you won't find leftovers in the refrigerator if you get the munchies late in the evening.

Most Americans do not shop daily nor twice-weekly. Most Americans shop as if they still lived on the frontier and had to take the pack mules 50 miles to the trading post to lay in supplies. Even when most of us live a mile or two from a good supermarket.

Of course, much of that food Americans cart home they did not intend to buy. A CNN business news report quoted that 43 percent of American supermarket purchases are impulse buying. Of course, very sophisticated marketing techniques prompt those impulse purchases. An even greater percentage of convenience store purchases are unplanned.

Impulse purchases are rarely for a package of alfalfa sprouts or some nice frozen green beans. And when Americans get those impulse purchases home, there are two things that they can do with them: Throw them out—the same as throwing away cash. Or eat them.

The French are not impulse shoppers. Besides most French houses and apartments lack any place to store impulse purchases when they get them home.

French kitchens have much less cabinet space than American kitchens. They don't need it. What about storage for mixes, baking supplies, cereals, cookies, crackers, frozen dinners and desserts— those items that hogged space in my cabinets and freezers in my fat days? The French breakfast is invariably bread with coffee, hot chocolate, or tea. The French cook from scratch; they eat fresh produce, not canned. They usually leave baking breads, cakes, pies, pastries, and cookies to the professionals. These bakery items are made without preservatives and eaten the day purchased.

## 500 CALORIES OF CAKE BATTER

I remember an afternoon tea attended by British, French, and American women. A British woman and an American woman seated near me were discussing baking. I saw the chic French woman nearby frowning. Finally she broke into their conversation. "You Americans and English," she scolded. "All you talk about is recipes. If I want a cake, I go to the *pâtisserie.*"

I looked at the French woman. A perfect size 2, dressed in that perfectly pressed way they always manage; her makeup was artfully applied. I thought of all the cakes I had baked, how many excess calories of batter I had licked from the beaters. I thought of the leftover cakes that seduced me to sliver a piece whenever I went in the kitchen.

Even when they do bake, French women are able to buy exact quantities of the ingredients they need for a *tarte* or *gâteau.* *Voilà!* No need to clutter up your cupboard with extra flour, sugar and such. No ingredients remain on hand to whip up a batch of *Macarons au Chocolat.*

The French have many household arrangement strategies that prevent snacking. For instance, their small refrigerators often have no place for storing a container of ice cream that puts the pounds on so many Americans in before-bedtime snacking.

Anyway, the French eat ice cream in ways that still strike me as peculiar. Often in rectangular slices. Or in a molded dessert called a *bombe*, the French word for our American word bomb—as in something that makes a big bang and blows up buildings.

The first time I heard an ice cream dessert called *une bombe*, I was dining in the home of some French people I knew only slightly. After the cheese course, I noticed the host going out the door. His wife said pleasantly, "Henri must go and pick up the bomb." For a shaky 15 minutes I feared I had been dining with terrorists.

But soon Henri returned from the pastry shop where the dessert ordered earlier had been kept in the shop's freezer. The ice cream creation was transported to the table on a lovely crystal plate where we admired it. But not for too long. The night was warm, so the *bombe* was quickly sliced, as a cake is sliced into wedge-shaped portions, and served. The portions were small; the slices equaled the number of guests. No second helpings, no leftovers, did you note?

### SOCIALIZING ON THEIR OWN TERMS

Contrary to what you often read, the French do entertain friends in their home. But such occasions are always planned and invitations issued days, if not a week in advance. Impromptu drop-ins are not a French thing to do.

Yet the French are extremely gregarious. Cafés and bistros are places to meet friends—when one decides one wants company. Not when the company decides to visit you.

For the French, their apartment or house is a sanctuary, a place where they can retreat without fear of being disturbed. Even a village too small to rate a café has a bench or low wall where it is customary to position yourself if you wish to encounter your acquaintances. Since people don't "drop by," you have no excuse to stock extra food in case they might. That excuse is the one so many Americans make for keeping extra food on hand.

## *LA DÉCO*

French women approach *la deco*, interior decoration, differently than Americans. When I first visited homes of French acquaintances, I felt sorry for them. Compared with Americans, they didn't have much "stuff." At that time my basic American mentality of "the more stuff the better" was well intact. Later I realized how minimizing furniture and decorating items to essentials saved French women work—and inches on their hips.

In the elegantly beautiful book, *French Style*, the authors, Suzanne Slesin and Stafford Cliff, explain that French women employ the same philosophy in decorating their homes as they do in dressing themselves in that chic, stylish manner we admire. French interiors, like chic French women, appear to be the product of a certain magic. They appear casual, yet they maintain an air of refined elegance. They are tranquil, yet never dull. They include classic, traditional elements, but they aren't boringly formal.

A French woman allows the decoration of her home to evolve, in the same manner she evolves a personal style. She might begin with necessity purchases for her first apartment, add something from an aunt's attic and a couple of marvelous finds at the *marché des puces*. French women rarely furnish a house the way many Americans do: go to a furniture store and have the store's decorator 'do' the room.

French women make housework easy for themselves. Kitchens and bathrooms look bare compared to those in American homes. But they are far easier to maintain. Decorator pieces in those rooms, like a French woman's fashion accessories, are few. And absolutely right.

Monastic is the term often used to describe the decor of French bedrooms. The French rarely bother with frilly bedspreads or decorator items on the walls. Beds often are platform style holding a mattress, but no box springs. Usually there is no headboard. Wooden shutters—not curtains or drapes—provide privacy.

My description of French home interiors as bare and monastic may surprise you. You may have the idea, as I once had, that French homes were decorated in either an elegant, formal Louis style or an only slightly less formal version we know in the USA as "French Provincial." (This style is not to be confused with the more recently popular French country style that takes inspiration from the Provence region of southern France.)

I remember a newspaper advertisement for a "Classic French Accent Chair with Louis XV styling." The advertisement went on to describe the chair's "floral and vinery carvings" and padded back and arms covered in a "rich jewel tone tapestry."

This is not the kind of chair a man sprawls back in with a Budweiser and watches the NFL playoffs.

When I read that French chair ad, I tried to remember if I had ever seen such a chair in a French home. All I remembered were chairs of the Euro Modern style, utilitarian but comfortable.

And once I attended a dinner party at the home of a slightly impoverished young French couple who took the back seat out of their Citroën *Deux Chevaux* and toted it upstairs to their apartment in order to have sufficient seating for their guests.

### THE FRENCH KITCHEN

Traditionally the French kitchen has been off-limits except for those individuals involved in food preparation. But I understand that in the past few years kitchens have begun to play a role in French life closer to the one the room plays in America. I hear the French are entertaining guests in their kitchens. And I see a potential for trouble. Fat trouble.

The problem with cozy, comfortable, TV-equipped American kitchens where the whole family, including pets, hangs out—and where guests come for a visit—is that food is always conveniently accessible. Too conveniently. Simply being in the kitchen, the designated "food room" of the house, makes a person vulnerable to the continual psychological suggestion to eat.

## *LE BOUDOIR*

I am convinced boudoirs are a chief reason French women don't use food as a stress reliever the way I did in my fat days.

In the beginning I had a major misconception about boudoirs. Somewhere I had picked up the notion they were rooms for sex. Illicit sex, at that. The irony, I found, is that a boudoir's function is a room where a woman can be alone. The word comes from the French *bouder* meaning to sulk or to pout. A boudoir is a room in which to sulk. In reality, it is a sanctuary where a French woman may seclude and restore herself. When a chic French woman feels frazzled and needs time alone, she retires to her boudoir.

Boudoirs perform the same useful function as pretty lingerie: making a French woman feel pampered and good about herself. American women, even when allocating time to themselves, feel compelled by their Puritan legacy to "do something productive." A chic French woman, however, feels totally comfortable doing nothing more than reclining on her chaise longue, staring out the window watching the rain, or reading poetry.

Biographer Judith Thurman, while at work on a book about the French author Colette, explained the French boudoir in *Victoria* magazine. She called it a French woman's form of nourishment and respectful self-indulgence. She describes the boudoir of a Parisian friend with its tiny marble fireplace and French doors opening onto a little balcony with boxes of ivy and geranium spilling over the wrought-iron railing. Sounded perfectly delightful and restorative to me.

## THAT BIDET: WHAT'S IT FOR ANYWAY?

Like French kitchens, bathrooms are usually plain and devoid of the kitschy decorator items often found in American bathrooms. No crocheted toilet tissue roll covers in French bathrooms. French bathrooms, however, come equipped with one appliance missing from most American bathrooms: the bidet.

How do you explain a bidet to someone who has never seen one? A newspaper decorating column contained the following sentence: "Common in Europe, the bidet is handy for foot baths and other localized cleansing as a water-saving option to drawing a full bath." I am certain the bidet plays a role in keeping French women slim. I have just never figured out exactly what role.

## TAKING A *PAS BELLE* DAY

The French actress Catherine Deneuve was quoted in an interview in *Vogue* several years ago, saying that if she had an "ugly" day she simply canceled everything for that day. How very French. Your hair frizzes, you develop a hang nail, you feel depressed; then, just say no, you aren't coming. Stay home and pamper yourself on a *pas belle* day.

What does pampering yourself have to do with keeping your hips slim?

Weight control therapists struggle to convince female patients to care for themselves and to believe they are worthy of that care. Overweight American women are often what I call "martyrs-in-training." Martyrs-in-training believe that everyone else is more important than they are: they believe they must be slaves to family and friends. When these martyrs-in-training's efforts on behalf of others aren't appreciated as these women believe they should be, they become angry and hurt. They salve that anger and hurt with high-calorie comfort food.

## HOUSE WORK

French women organize their households in a simpler fashion than American women because French women are more realistic about men. I decided years ago that the reason French bathrooms never have many towel racks is that French women don't expect their husbands to pick up their wet towels anyway!

I believe the reason so many French families live in apartments is that French women know it is easier to get the Arabs and the Israelis to the negotiating table than to persuade a husband to clean out the garage and mow the lawn. In France if you want grass, fresh air, and trees, you go to the park—which some uniformed French civil servant keeps trimmed and tidy. Besides, a French woman would not expect Jean-Claude or Roger to give up his Saturday afternoons in the café talking politics or his regular game of boules for house and yard work.

Even when the French home is surrounded by a yard, the yard rarely has grass. More likely a vegetable and herb garden fills the area. Or the ground is graveled. Flowers grow in pots on a terrace. Look in the house and garden magazines, you find that even the grounds of a French chateau are graveled.

French women organize their households in a manner that minimizes the time they must spend on meal preparation, shopping, cleaning, and yard maintenance. The simpler the household, the less chance for stressful occurrences—and the less chance for disputes with a husband because he fails to help around the house.

Less house and yard work also means less fatigue. Exhaustion, American doctors tell us, is the most common complaint that they hear. From my own experience and from observations of overweight American women, I think much excess calorie consumption is for energy to combat the exhaustion that comes with their busy, stressful lives. French women have wisely set up systems of shopping and household management that minimize their fatigue and distress—and maximize their pleasure. The pay-off is a slim waistline.

We come finally to the last factor that keeps those chic French women slim: their relationship with men. Here the difference between American and French women gapes widest.

## *Praise for Chic & Slim*

I guarantee if you love French culture, foods and the *je ne sais quoi* about the women in France, you'll love this book. You might find yourself transforming yourself into a chic American woman (or Canadian, Irish, etc.) who knows the secrets that were once owned solely by French women. Thanks to Anne Barone, those secrets are accessible to all of us. She should know, she's studied the differences and used them in her own life to keep herself chic and slim for over 30 years.

— ANNE CERVA writing in her review of
*Chic & Slim Encore* on her French Cuisine website
*frenchfood.about.com*

# CHAPTER SIX

# L'Amour & La Vie

## LESS CONFRONTATION IN LOVE & LIFE HELPS FRENCH WOMEN STAY CHIC & SLIM

*France is the only country in the world where men and women really understand each other.*

The claim, made by French writer and former editor of the French *Elle*, Françoise Giroud, was quoted in Sanche de Gramont's book *The French*. A quarter century later Madame Giroud still believed French men and women maintain a unique level of understanding. She told the American edition of *Elle* she believes relations between men and women in France remain the best in the world—even if they aren't always paradise.

Relationships in France have their problems, as do those everywhere on the planet. But French women aren't caught up, as American women are, in how men should be. They accept how men are. *Quelle différence!*

This acceptance saves French women the grief and frustration that sends American women searching for comfort in food. When I consider French women's equanimity toward the inevitable problems in relationships, I think of that line in a song French *chanteuse* Edith Piaf used to belt out about paying *de temps en temps des larmes*—paying from time to time with tears—in order to be allowed to love.

If, despite occasional tears, relations between French men and women are the best in the world, how would those between American men and women rank? Probably like our high school math scores: below the rest of the industrialized world, but slightly higher than Lesotho.

## THE BIG IRONY

The irony is that divorce rates are as high in France as in the USA; French men are notorious for their adultery—and French women are known to dabble in their own *projets d'amour* outside the bounds of marriage. Relationships end with heartbreak as they do in the USA. The difference seems to be that, in France, men and women don't say as many mean things to each other in the process. They certainly don't shoot at each other as often.

If the battle between the sexes in France inflicts less mental and physical wounding than in America, it is probably because of the different views of love and marriage in France and the USA.

The idea that marriage is based on love and will bring everlasting happiness to the partners is an American notion. Actually, we are about the only country where men and women put such heavy expectations on the institution. The French put fewer demands on marriage. But they have extraordinary expectations for *l'amour*. For the French, love is as necessary as food.

For the French, a love affair is more than just sex. As much thought and effort goes into the preparation and execution of a romance as into a well-prepared French meal. A love affair begins with flirtation, an hors d'oeuvre, that whets the appetite for more. Just as the French prefer to take time to anticipate and enjoy their meals, they prefer that romance should be anticipated, then a leisurely progress made through its several stages. Each stage is savored and given the participants's full attention. (As in don't take your mobile phone to the bedroom.) To the French, the main course, sex, is something exquisite: an art, as cerebral as it is physical.

American women have nothing against the French approach to romance and sex. Trying to get American men to participate in this approach is another matter. It would probably be easier to strap wings on the Statue of Liberty and teach her to fly.

## IT AIN'T EASY, SISTERS

Unfortunately, many American women's efforts to organize delicious little romantic interludes turn out much as the one Erma Bombeck described in her column titled "Romance is dead—especially when it stops at my patio." Erma served an elegant, romantic breakfast for two on her terrace. Instead of eating, her husband kept popping up to water plants and do lawn chores. He didn't like the breakfast she prepared and wouldn't eat it. Erma's punch line rang too true: "I ate all of his breakfast and mine, too."

If American women are angry and frustrated by American men, and if this frustration is driving them to overeat, it may be for some darn good reasons.

But why are American men so uncomfortable with those little romantic interludes which are standard operating procedure for French men and women? Is it the Puritan ethic coming into play and they don't feel comfortable doing something pleasurable? If so, where was that Puritanical guilt the weekend they spent at the golf tournament? Could it be American impatience? Then why don't American men become impatient the endless hours they spend tinkering with the engine of their car?

The difference is that, whether inside marriage or outside it, the French are more willing to see relationships as comprised of mutual obligations. French women have an obligation to please men with their appearance and adoration. French men respond with those small gestures of consideration that mean so much to women. And relationships in France involve less confrontation than in America.

## VIVE LA DIFFÉRENCE

Several years ago an article comparing relationships in the USA with those in France appeared in *The New York Times Magazine*. In "Vive la Différence" American writer Mark Hunter explained that in 1982, at age 30, he moved to Paris. He says at that time American male-female relationships were competitive and combative. (Don't know if you've been back lately, Mr. Hunter, but they still are.) Real life conversations sounded like the traded insults in a comedy television series.

I always remember the episode of *Moonlighting* where the Bruce Willis character asked the Cybill Shepherd character to go out with him, and she turned him down saying she would rather stay home and recaulk the bathtub. Such remarks make clever sitcom dialogue. But in real life those insults hurt badly. In real life many insults hurled at American women in combative exchanges are derogatory criticisms of their bodies. Those hurtful criticisms can be disastrous for weight control.

In Paris, Mark Hunter was delighted to find relationships less grisly than in the USA. So much less grisly that he married a French woman. He commented that his very feminine French wife expected and received from him small, considerate gestures. In exchange she gave him care and acknowledgement. It was old-fashioned, Mr. Hunter admitted, but for them it was satisfactory and workable.

I hear American feminists wailing. For decades they have preached that men are the enemy who brainwash us into prettying ourselves up to earn their approval. Can somebody give a better reason for all the time, effort, and money spent?

## FRUITS OF FRUSTRATION

In America, frustration with husbands and lovers drives many women to seek counseling. Others buy books and magazines with advice on how to cope with problems and improve relationships. The advice often aims at changing and reforming men. A magazine cover blurb for a how-to article I once saw purported to explain to American women how to get their husbands to pick up their dirty socks.

I can't imagine a sock-picking-up article in a French magazine. French women realize that men, by their nature and biology, neither readily change nor reform. French women waste little effort aimed toward husbands picking up their socks. Nor do French women spend time nagging husbands to wash their hair more often or change from the wrinkled shirts and slacks they have worn for several days. (French men do tend toward rumpled clothes and greasy hair.) French wives are equally understanding about male memory.

An American woman expects her husband will remember their anniversary. When he doesn't, she is hurt and angry and exacts a penalty from him. Frequently this penalty takes the form of rejecting and spoiling whatever he offers as penance for this lapse. A foolish and self-defeating move on her part.

French women, on the other hand, know that without gentle prompting, husbands forget birthdays and anniversaries. A week before the event, Madeline will say over the dinner *boeuf bourguignon*, "Jean-Claude, I was thinking that for our anniversary how lovely it would be to have dinner at that very romantic little restaurant you took me to last year. Should I call and make a reservation for Friday evening?" (Note that she is specific as to the day of the anniversary. She avoids any hint that she thinks he hasn't remembered.) At this point Jean-Claude says gallantly in his grumbly Gauloises-thickened voice, "Ah, non, *Chérie*. I will make the reservations."

Jean-Claude has his reminder with no damage done to his ego. Madeline gets dinner in a romantic restaurant with no arguments or hostile words to mar her anniversary.

## REALITY TIME

French women's realistic acceptance of men's basic natures holds many French relationships together. Thus, French women avoid the exhausting and depressing loneliness responsible for many American women gaining weight after a breakup.

True, American women may, in a frenzy of dieting, lose weight immediately after the breakup. But shortly after their former partner finds someone new (someone younger and slimmer), the frustration eating begins and pounds start settling on the hips.

A French wife may be unhappy that her husband is having an extramarital affair, but she will see this as a perfectly natural thing to happen. If he takes a mistress, likely she will not divorce him for it. Not unless she is looking for a handy excuse.

A French wife certainly will not allow a husband's infidelities to take a toll on her appearance. She may simply decide that what is good for the gander is good for the goose. She may take a lover herself. Frequently a man younger than herself.

Instead of trying to make her lover think she is younger than she actually is, a French woman will play on the age difference to seduce him with the promise of her greater expertise and experience in sexual matters. You have to hand it to them, French women have figured all the angles.

Too, the French attitude toward sex remains sufficiently detached and refined that love affairs avoid much of the messy aftermath that follows breakups in America.

## THE WAY IT WORKS

French women's realistic acceptance of men's basic natures makes for relationships in which mutual respect and support are the foundation. French women don't worry about being "equal." French women don't want to be equal. They want to be feminine, desirable, happy. They want to eat well, and enjoy art, nature, their families, and the month of August for a holiday.

American women have decided they want to be the same as men: equal. This isn't happening, so a lot of American women are angry at American men. Men don't understand the anger; they don't like the change in the system. A lot of confusion and frustration exists on both sides.

French women and men acknowledge that men and women are different. They have worked out a system based on acceptance of these differences.

## NOTICE

Please understand that accepting men as they are in NO WAY advocates putting up with physical or verbal abuse. Accepting that men leave wet towels on the bathroom floor and that they prefer watching football to mowing the lawn is one thing. Suffering abuse is another. Do not accept abuse.

## TRUTH OR FICTION?

Another reason the relationships between French men and women are better than those of their American counterparts is the French approach to truth. Several years ago in America we experienced a push for honesty in relationships. This was not necessarily a step forward.

For the French, charming, well-told little fictions can provide the lubrication that keeps a relationship running smoothly. Holly Brubach writing "In Fashion" from Paris for *The New Yorker* said that honesty is not so highly prized in France as in America. That is not accusing the French of dishonesty. But for them, creative little fictions are a means of expression.

French fashion designer Sonia Rykiel told Jean Bond Rafferty in an interview for *Town & Country* that she didn't know what it was not to lie—and she says she lies very well. Her little fictions never aim to hurt anyone. Rather, she tells them because they are prettier and more interesting than the truth.

French men and women are experts in crafting and delivering little fictions. And they do it in their own self-interest—to the delight of their partners. And for the success of their relationships.

**THE GAME OF LOVE**

But an overdose of honesty has a far smaller negative impact on American relationships than the pervasiveness in our culture of the sports mentality. Instead of synergistic partnerships French men and women strive for, Americans turn every relationship into a contest. Both sides keep score. Both sides are conscious of their ranking. Somebody has to win and somebody has to lose. The French value romance more highly than competition; both partners in a relationship come out winners.

**MOTIVATION TO STAY SLIM**

Staying slim and attractive takes effort—even when Nature has been generous. And the more years of a woman's life that pass, the more effort it seems to take to stay slim and attractive. Something must motivate a woman to continue making that effort morning after morning, year after year, decade after decade.

In the USA today, a woman staying slim and attractive for men is out of fashion. In recent decades many books and magazine articles have advised that a woman should be motivated to lose weight for her own sake. If the test is in the results, looking at the relatively better job French women do at staying slim for men than American women do for themselves, you've got to admit that the men motivation appears to achieve better results.

Could medical science ever concoct a more powerful appetite suppressant than falling in love? This question leads to another problem for weight control in America.

## FAT AS PROTECTION

All across America, morning after morning, struggling into their queen size panty hose are married American women who fear if they lose weight and become more attractive, they will be tempted to have an affair. They believe fat protects them from propositions. For some reason it does not occur to these otherwise intelligent women that you don't have to accept every proposition you get. You can "Just Say No," as we keep telling the kids about illegal drugs.

Scores of American husbands sabotage their wives's weight loss attempts because they are afraid that if a wife becomes more attractive, she will no longer be content with her fat slob of a husband. One cannot entirely refute these fears.

Yet wouldn't it make more sense for the husband to participate in his wife's efforts at improving eating and exercise habits? It does not occur to either husbands or wives that they might lose excess fat for the mate they already have—or for health reasons. Or that they might want to be slim and to dress attractively not, in quest of some carnal passion, but for aesthetic reasons.

## MYSELF, A WORK OF ART

Aesthetics are highly valued in France. Beauty and art have long been a part of French culture. The French have created some of the world's most treasured architecture, paintings, literature, drama, music, and sculpture. When you travel in France, in every region you find not only spectacular natural scenery, but beautiful castles and cathedrals, museums filled with art, concert halls and theaters presenting excellent musical programs and drama.

In this inspiring milieu, French women have come to view themselves as works of art. They believe their attractive appearance brings pleasure to others, just as does a well-designed chateau, a lyrical sonata, or an inspiring painting. So what if men flirt and whisper suggestions? French women learn early how to deal with men's advances so they can either accept or refuse with the same charm and grace.

Few American women learn this art of refusal with charm and grace. Furthermore, American women are made to feel that, if they are attractive and a man makes an unwanted advance, that advance indicates they are bad women "who asked for it." This Puritan mentality has the French shaking their heads and saying, *"Ils sont fous, ces Américains."* They are crazy, those Americans.

You can usually count a Frenchman's expression of interest as a compliment. But often in America, a proposition expresses a man's contempt for a woman. (Actually what it expresses is his really screwed-up sexuality.) At the same time, many American women interpret any compliment from a man as sexual harassment.

American women become angry and upset when men consider them a "sex object." French women become angry and upset if men *don't* consider them a "sex object."

Austrian-born, Academy Award-winning actor Maximilian Schell settled a sexual harassment lawsuit by a woman producer who claimed he had, among other things, made graphic comments about her body in front of other people. Schell, in his sixties, said, "All I said was that she has beautiful breasts. In Europe, thank god, that is still a compliment."

French women don't interpret compliments on their body or clothes as harassment. They see them as confirmation they are succeeding in their goal of being attractive to men. On the other hand, sexual harassment in America is real. No one likes leers, slimy references to our anatomy, being patted, pinched, or rubbed against. I am disturbed that many American women, either consciously or unconsciously, choose excess fat as protection against unwanted attentions from men.

Part of the education of French women in *l'art de femme* is learning how to handle unwanted advances. Much of that haughtiness of which French women are accused is, I think, a setting of boundaries. At the same time, as I said previously, French women are expert in tact and graciousness in refusing advances by men. There would be fewer overweight women in the United States if American women would learn methods other than body fat for protecting themselves from unwanted advances and sexual harassment. There are other ways. An example follows.

## THE TALE OF JACK THE UNZIPPER

Back in the Dark Ages of the 1950s—back before women's defense classes and assertiveness training—there was a man in my hometown I shall call Jack the Unzipper. Women's fashion in those days meant dresses with long neck-to-below-the-waist zippers. And Jack the Unzipper's personal variety of sexual harassment was to slip up behind a woman busy in the office or in conversation at a party and unzip her dress. In the Puritanical 1950s this unzipping embarrassed and distressed the local women.

But one night at a party, Jack picked the wrong victim. This particular woman believed in equality of the sexes. When she felt the zipper of her dress sliding down, she whirled around and grabbed the zipper on Jack's trousers. And she yanked. The zipper caught the cotton of Jack's boxer shorts. It also caught the skin of a very sensitive part of his anatomy. And before zipper, shorts, and skin got sorted out, Jack experienced great physical pain.

That night marked the end of the career of Jack the Unzipper.

## WHAT MAKES THE DIFFERENCE?

So why do French women perceive men and their actions so differently than American women do? Is there something special about French men that make French women content and willing to please them?

For one thing, French men perform thoughtful gestures that make women feel feminine and appreciated. I saw an excellent example of a Frenchman's thoughtfulness in a CNN "Style" segment on a Parisian fashion photography session. When the time came for the model to go in front of the lights, the French photographer escorted her from the dressing table to the camera in the courtly manner one would escort an 18th century French queen.

You can imagine an American photographer in the same situation working with the settings on his camera and growling, "Okay, get over here, honey."

French men practice courtesy in a hundred small ways, but for centuries the ultimate courtesy of French men toward French women has been the French male's willing acceptance of principal responsibility for birth control.

## THE ULTIMATE COURTESY

The French male developed *coitus interruptus* to an art form long before more medically sophisticated forms of contraception existed. In the 19th century, French male economists encouraged French women to limit their families as a way of making their lives easier and more financially prosperous. As a result, the French birth rate was low, particularly low for a country more than 85 percent Roman Catholic.

The courtesy continues. It was, after all, a French male doctor who developed RU-486, the nonsurgical remedy for unwanted pregnancy.

That does not mean, however, that the French are anti-baby. It was Dr. Fernand Lamaze, another French male doctor, who developed the well-known Lamaze method of natural childbirth that caused a revolution in birthing procedures in the USA, as well as in France. Thanks to Dr. Lamaze, babies are born more safely. Fathers are no longer excluded from their children's birth, but present and supportive.

## THE MOST IMPORTANT MOTIVATION

Yet if you have to name the one factor that most motivates French women to stay slim and attractive, it is surely the attitude of French men—and French society in general—toward older women. In France they don't say a middle-aged woman or an older woman. They say, *une femme d'un certain âge*. A woman of a certain age. And no one has to be too certain what that age is.

French actress Catherine Deneuve told Jon Wilde for an article published in *Mirabella* that she believes it is easier for a woman to get old in Europe than in America. She surmises this is because in Europe charm is highly valued, while in the USA it is not.

No, charm is not valued highly in the USA. Nor do most Americans value *la femme mûre*, the ripe woman, who is as revered in France as a fine aged wine. Actresses such as Catherine Deneuve, in her sixties at this writing, who earned a Best Actress Oscar nomination for her role as the passionate French colonial in the 1992 French film *Indochine*; Jeanne Moreau, who in her sixties played the elegantly flamboyant Anglo-Egyptian in the 1993 *The Summer House*; and Anouk Aimée, who in her fifties played a leading role in Robert Altman's 1994 *Prêt-à-Porter*, were as sought after for staring roles as when they were making classics like *Belle de Jour* (1967 Deneuve), *The Lovers* (1958 Moreau), and *A Man and a Woman* (1966 Aimée). In France the older woman is admired for her experience. She is attractive to men her own age, as well as to men many years younger.

Because a French woman knows she will be appreciated in her forties, fifties—even in her eighties—she takes care of herself and keeps herself slim and attractive.

Whatever her age, a French woman makes the effort to look attractive for men—even when the relationships between men and women aren't always paradise.

A French *femme d'un certain âge* once complained to me with exasperation, "Men! Sometimes they can be so maddening." Then she shrugged and added philosophically, "But life without them would be like a day without bread."

French women find it easier to stay chic and slim than American women. French women live in a culture that aids and encourages them in the process. They organize their households so that they maximize time for caring for their families and themselves and minimize conflict with spouses over the household chores. French women see great value in a unique personal style— for self-satisfaction and as a means to satisfying relationships. They believe in the time and effort necessary to be healthy and attractive because they have a strong aesthetic sense and the desire to make themselves a living, breathing work of art that they and others enjoy.

French women have perfected a marvelous system that allows them to enjoy French bread—and the rest of their rich French cuisine—yet still stay chic and slim.

*Fantastique!*

# Chic & Slim Anywhere

Now you know those chic French secrets.

Now you know how those chic French women eat all that rich food and still stay slim. And how they dress so chic.

You also have an idea of the forces fueling the obesity epidemic. Seductive snack foods lurk everywhere. Food advertising manipulates you to hunger. Food pushers tantalize you with second helpings. Nouveaux Puritans warn you that everything tasty is bad for your health. Fitness gurus prescribe exercise programs for which you lack both the time and energy.

You battle the Fat Monster in a competitive culture that tries to label 20 extra pounds as proof of moral failing. This same culture worships whatever is biggest. Quantity rates louder applause than quality.

Is it really possible to lose weight and stay slim today?

Yes! *Mais oui!*

I believe passionately that almost anyone, no matter where they live, can achieve and maintain a healthy weight—and still eat the foods they love. I did. I do. You just have to know how.

The *how* is my Chic & Slim translation of French women's techniques.

During the past four decades, I have tailored that translation to work for me whether I was living in the United States (even here in the barbecue and enchilada culture of Texas) or abroad.

Certainly your genetic heritage plays a role in determining whether your figure naturally tends toward the silhouette of a string bean or a cream puff. Yet I know from my own experience, and from observing hundreds of others, that how you feel about yourself ultimately plays a greater role than genes in whether you are chic and slim or frumpy and dumpy. Being overweight is not so much about what you eat as about *why you overeat.*

*Ultimately, staying slim is not about counting calories or fat grams. Staying slim is not about exercise exhaustion. Staying slim is really about personal style. Fashion is about clothes. Personal style is an approach to Life.*

You can lose weight and stay slim. Unhappiness and health problems resulting from excess weight are unnecessary. My life has been so much richer and happier since I lost weight. I feel so fortunate to have discovered French women's techniques—and to have devised a system so that a fatty from fried chicken and pecan pie country could use them successfully. I wrote this book to share with you what those chic French women shared with me.

In the next section—The Anne Barone 100—are techniques I use to make the French system work for me wherever I am.

Some of the "100" have to do with lifestyle. Others have to do with eating. Good food is such joy. Who wants a weight control system that denies you the pleasure of eating well? What I learned from French women is that you do not have to deny yourself delicious food in order to be slim. You can eat well and still look as *fantastique* as those chic French women.

If you know how.

# *The Anne Barone 100*

## 100 FRENCH TECHNIQUES TO MAKE YOU CHIC & SLIM

1. Eat real food, not "diet" food.

2. Socialize with slim people. You will see their good habits.

3. Eat only when seated.

4. Take small bites. Chew slowly and completely.

5. Develop or refine your own personal style.

6. Get adequate sleep. Exhaustion leads to eating for energy.

7. Sell at resale or give to charity any clothing that doesn't fit or doesn't make you look attractive.

8. Identify the thing you hate most and stop doing it.

9. Eat meals in courses.

10. Wear lingerie that makes you feel pretty and special.

11. Pick a role model: someone slim whose values and lifestyle you admire. Study how they eat, dress, live, and relax.

12. Never eat when you are angry or upset.

13. Eat at meals. Don't snack between meals.

14. Make a survey of hidden sugar are you eating in condiments and processed food.

15. Eat breads made without fats, sugars, chemicals, or preservatives. Eat bread without butter except for breakfast.

16. Find something you enjoy more than eating—and do it regularly.

17. Don't eat while you watch television.

18. Eat fresh, high-quality fruits and vegetables.

19. Don't eat breakfast the minute you hop out of bed. You will be hungry for a mid-morning snack.

20. Cut down on the amount of food you keep in your home.

21. For best taste and nutrition, make a salad immediately before serving. Let everyone add their own salad dressing.

22. NEVER buy clothing in a size too small with the idea that you will diet to fit it. Buy clothes that fit well and that you can wear the day of purchase and look great.

23. Substitute mineral water or tap water with a squeeze of lemon or lime for carbonated soft drinks.

24. Be conscious of food advertising. Ask yourself if your hunger is real, or only a response to advertising suggestion.

25. Eat fresh fruit without sugar.

26. Don't buy high-calorie snack foods. If they aren't in the house, you can't eat them when you get the midnight munchies.

27. Try new low-calorie vegetable recipes.

28. Take at least 20 minutes every day just for yourself.

29. Make sandwiches open face. Eat them with knife and fork.

30. Replace commercial salad dressings with a vinaigrette from good quality olive oil and vinegar.

31. Organize a boudoir that is off-limits to other family members. Make it your sanctuary against the stresses of life.

32. Wear form-fitting clothes that signal any weight gain.

33. If you lose five pounds and someone says you look sick, tell them you are sick. Tell them you are sick of malicious people

who say that you look sick every time you make some progress toward a healthy weight. Tell them you are on your way to better health.

34. Plant a *potager*, a French-style kitchen garden.

35. Read articles and books about chic French women.

36. Don't make relationships one big "Who's Right?" contest.

37. If you drink iced tea, limit tea with caffeine to 1 or 2 glasses per day. Learn to drink herbal teas iced and hot.

38. Say no to exploitative people. No excuses. Just say no.

39. Stay out of the kitchen unless you are preparing meals.

40. Spend time with people who make you laugh.

41. Make five improvements in household organization that cut down on housework.

42. Avoid people who trample your self-esteem.

43. Take a low-calorie vegetable dish or salad to a family dinner. Fill your plate with a large portion of your low-calorie vegetables, take small amounts of high-calorie dishes.

44. Don't buy into the negativity. Believe you CAN lose weight and stay slim. And you will.

45. To cure a fast food obsession, regularly pick up litter in parks or on beaches. You will begin to loathe those logos.

46. Leave an abusive relationship.

47. Don't talk about your menopause symptoms except with your doctor or closest friend. It spoils your mystique.

48. To be satisfied with smaller portions, avoid pre-eaten foods. Instead of fish sticks, eat baked fish with bones to remove. Instead of fruit cup, eat fresh fruit you must peel.

49. Watch French films to see how chic French women eat.

50. Avoid people who consistently overeat and who are only interested in food-focused activities.

51. Regularly treat yourself to a facial or bubble bath.

52. Keep a carton of low-calorie soup in the freezer as your "fast food" when you are too busy to cook.

53. Don't bake desserts. Buy only enough for one serving per person with no leftovers.

54. For a holiday dinner, buy and prepare only three-fourths as much food as usual. Donate the money saved to the Salvation Army, local food bank, or feed-the-homeless organization.

55. Avoid people you don't like.

56. Learn to identify quality fruit and vegetables.

57. Go to France and see how chic French women eat & dress.

58. If you always overeat at family dinners, visit by telephone.

59. Spend your food money on quality food, not on advertising hype and packaging.

60. Give up trying to control other people.

61. Hit the mute button when food advertising comes on TV. Shut your eyes.

62. Read a book or magazine article about dressing slim.

63. Instead of weighing yourself on a bathroom scale, have a benchmark piece of clothing to monitor your size.

64. Tell a little white lie if it makes someone feel good.

65. Find a good source of artisan bread or learn to bake good bread without chemicals and preservatives.

66. Dance more, sit less.

67. Invest in a salad spinner. Salad will taste better.

68. Read or reread Peter Mayle's delightful books about France.

69. Post a neat CHEW SLOWLY sign on your table.

70. Indulge yourself once a week in a meal at which you don't worry about calories or nutrition. Eat, but don't overeat.

71. Give up dry breakfast cereals. Breakfast cereals are not chic.

72. Don't tolerate offensive behavior.

73. Replace mayonnaise with French Dijon mustard.

74. Keep in mind three foolproof answers for food pushers.

75. Eat elegantly from china or earthenware dishes with silver or stainless tableware. Use cloth napkins.

76. Smuggle your own air-popped, lightly-salted popcorn into the movie theater. Big purses are useful.

77. Plant herbs in your backyard or in pots on your windowsill. Cook with more herbs and less salt.

78. Avoid packaged foods, instant products, and mixes. You are worth real food.

79. Limit alcohol to a moderate amount of wine with meals.

80. Use naps as French women do for restoring energy and beauty.

81. Don't tolerate sexual harassment.

82. Sing a lot. You can't sing and eat at the same time.

83. To halt obsessive eating, throw the food you are stuffing into your mouth into the garbage disposer and hit the switch. Leave the food area.

84. Make your relationships less confrontational and combative, more synergistic.

85. Instead of lunch, meet friends for coffee or tea.

86. Request non-food gifts.

87. Learn to make Parisian-style French onion soup.

88. Go outside in the fresh air at least one half-hour daily.

89. Always keep one package of frozen green beans on hand. When you are too tired to prepare a meal for yourself, cook the beans, garnish with lemon juice and 1 teaspoon olive oil. Eat them with good bread for an easy, low-calorie meal.

90. Find some exercise you enjoy and do it regularly.

91. Enjoy a relaxing afternoon tea.

92. Always let cheese warm to room temperature before eating. Taste will be better. Cheese will spread more easily. You will eat less, but enjoy more.

93. Don't bore people talking about your efforts at weight control. It spoils your mystique.

94. Learn to make jams and preserves as the French do using unsweetened grape or apple juice in place of sugar.

95. Never nibble while preparing food. If you taste to correct seasonings, spit it out.

96. Cut down on lawn mowing by converting areas to ground cover and mulched vegetable garden.

97. Eat small portions.

98. Work out anger by pulling weeds or pelting the bathtub with a wet, wadded wash cloth.

99. Don't attempt too many lifestyle changes too quickly.

100. Enjoy something RICH and FRENCH!

# More Books

## TO MAKE YOU FRENCH CHIC & SLIM

A Goose in Toulouse and other Culinary Adventures in France (Hyperion 2000) Mort Rosenblum. The state of food in France *circa* 2000 in a witty and entertaining book.

**Hotel Pastis: A Novel of Provence** (Knopf 1993) Peter Mayle. Nicole Bouvier is an excellent fictional portrait of a chic French woman who can eat all that rich food and still stay slim. She cooks well, too.

**A Year in Provence** (Vintage Books 1991) and **Toujours Provence** (Vintage Books 1992) Peter Mayle. Much information on the French personality, foods, shopping, and eating habits.

**Bobbi Brown Beauty** (HarperStyle 1997) Bobbi Brown & Annemarie Iverson. Guidance on the makeup element in your personal style.

**Women & Beauty** (William Morrow and Company 1984) Sophia Loren. Though Italian, the actress's philosophy toward mature beauty and her techniques for developing and maintaining it are much those of chic French women. "Some Thoughts On Beauty" outlines the role self-confidence plays in beauty.

**Bardot Deneuve Fonda: My Life With The Three Most Beautiful Women In The World** (Simon and Schuster 1986) Roger Vadim. Useful for weight control is the descriptions of the contrast in the way Brigitte Bardot (French) and Jane Fonda (American) approach food.

**Literary Women** (Doubleday 1976) Ellen Moers. The author devotes an entire chapter to Madame de Staël.

**French Chic** (Villard Books 1988) Susan Sommers. A classic book for understanding how French women develop their own personal style and the role it plays in their lives.

**AudreyStyle** (HarperCollins 1999) Pamela Clarke Keogh. A style biography of actress Audrey Hepburn whose personal style was the epitome of chic, elegant simplicity.

**French Style: How to Think, Shop and Dress Like A French Woman** (Express 1993) Véronique Vienne. The basics of French personal style.

**Chanel: A Woman of Her Own** (Henry Holt and Co. 1990) Axel Madsen. Biography of French fashion designer Coco Chanel explains her fashion philosophy that shaped the French approach to style.

**From Julia Child's Kitchen** (Knopf 1975) Julia Child. This book, along with the classic *Mastering the Art of French Cooking*, and any of the other books and videos by Julia Child are excellent guides to preparing French cuisine in the American kitchen.

**Patricia Wells At Home In France** (Scribner 1996) Patricia Wells. Cookbook and writer's life in her restored 18th century farmhouse in Provence.

**French Tea** (Hearst Books 1993) Carole Manchester. An elegant book on tea drinking in France. With recipes and lovely photos.

**French Style** (Clarkson N. Potter 1982) Suzanne Slesin & Stafford Cliff. French architecture and interior decoration.

**Chic & Slim Encore: More About How French Women Dress Chic Stay Slim—and How You Can Too** 2nd Edition (The Anne Barone Company 2009) Anne Barone. The second Chic & Slim book.

**Chic & Slim Techniques: 10 techniques to make you chic & slim *à la française*** (Nouvelles Editions 2002) Anne Barone. Easy techniques for a chic style and slim body *à la française*.

# Merci Beaucoup

With today's computer technology, a writer with a message can write, design, edit—even typeset—her book. Still, she needs real live people.

It is wonderful when family and friends willingly help. It is equally wonderful when women you have never met take an interest in your project and, like family and friends, take the time to read your manuscript, react, and make suggestions. I am deeply grateful to all who made time in their busy lives to help with this book.

As always, I am grateful to my son John for his understanding, support, and assistance on this project that has taken far longer than either of us imagined. I am also grateful to Jennifer Silber—not only for her excellent proofreading skills—but also for her extensive critique. (If there are errors in this book, the fault is totally that of the author because I made numerous revisions after the proofreading.)

Bobbye Scott was first to read the final version. Her positive reaction to the book came at a moment I desperately needed it. Nancy Benton generously shared her experiences living with a French roommate—and later with a French family. Her comments made this a better book. Susan Hicks also helped with proofreading and critique. Judy Eagle, Lorraine Stevenson, Betty Buchanan, and Dodie Hummell also gave useful feedback on the manuscript.

Ron Burt and Shirley Peddy, Ph.D. gave helpful advice on the techniques of independent publishing.

Joyce Wells created the Chic & Slim Eiffel Tower used on the back cover and on the Chic & Slim website *annebarone.com*.

Again, *merci*. Thanks to all of you.

# Au Revoir

As I was finishing the revisions to the second edition, I received an email from "Nancy in Hartford," in which she described an insight that had come after reading the second Chic & Slim book, *Chic & Slim Encore*:

> It dawned on me that the whole Chic & Slim concept is not one big change: *Voilà*, a new you! But rather a continuous series of small changes made daily, that will gradually refine, define, and finally become authentically you.

"Authentically you" is important. With Chic & Slim, you do not impose someone else's system on your life, but rather tailor the techniques to your unique needs and lifestyle. Change is gradual— and lasting. One reason "diets" do not work is that they require you to make too many changes at once. Mind and body revolt at all that disruption to the familiar.

No French woman believes she has defined her personal style until she is at least 30. Throughout her life, she continues to refine and improve that style.

You are a work of art. Your personal style is always a "work in progress" becoming better and more authentically you every year.

Most of all, enjoy the creation of your unique personal style. Find the pleasure, find the *joie de vivre* Chic & Slim.

be Chic, stay Slim,

Anne Barone

# More Chic & Slim Books

TO KEEP YOU AS CHIC AND SLIM
AS THOSE *OOH-LA-LA* FRENCH WOMEN

**THE SUPERCHARGER**
## CHIC & SLIM ENCORE:
MORE ABOUT FRENCH CHIC AND SLIM

**THE HOW-TO**
## CHIC & SLIM TECHNIQUES:
10 TECHNIQUES TO MAKE YOU CHIC & SLIM
*À LA FRANÇAISE*

**CHIC & SLIM FOREVER**
## CHIC & SLIM TOUJOURS:
AGING BEAUTIFULLY LIKE THOSE
CHIC FRENCH WOMEN

## CHIC & SLIM BOOKS BY ANNE BARONE
AVAILABLE FROM AMAZON, BARNESANDNOBLE.COM
AND OTHER BOOKSELLERS

## CHIC & SLIM BOOK ORDER INFORMATION
MORE FRENCH SECRETS & TECHNIQUES
ON THE CHIC & SLIM WEBSITE

# annebarone.com

CPSIA information can be obtained at www.ICGtesting.com
Printed in the USA
BVOW010116270712

296129BV00008B/7/P